MEDITE
VEGETABL

Rena Salaman, whose family originated in
Asia Minor, was born in German-occupied
Athens and grew up there amidst the civil
war that followed. For some years she
travelled as an air-hostess with Olympic
Airways, which gave her a taste of the world's
great cuisines. Married to an English aca-
demic, she settled in London, where they now
live with their twin daughters, while
spending each summer at the family home
in Greece.

Her previous books include *Greek Food*
(1983), *The Little Mediterranean Food Book* (1986),
The Cooking of Greece and Turkey (1987) and *Greek
Island Cooking* (1987). She has appeared on tele-
vision, and in numerous radio programmes.

MEDITERRANEAN VEGETABLE COOKERY

Rena Salaman

FONTANA/Collins

To my sisters Maria and Sally
for a shared Mediterranean upbringing.

First published in Great Britain by William Collins 1987
First issued in Fontana Paperbacks 1988

Copyright © Rena Salaman 1987

Printed and bound in Great Britain by
William Collins Sons & Co. Ltd, Glasgow

CONTENTS

ACKNOWLEDGEMENTS

The present book is the fruit of endless stimulating discussions (and arguments) with friends, over convivial, extended meals in true Mediterranean fashion, around that fabled sea, as well as in London. Primarily, though, it is owed to my grandmother and my mother for bestowing upon me an intimate and warm Mediterranean upbringing with their unique insight and knowledge and their tales about 'places past' – those visited and, occasionally, even those not visited; the colours, vividly painted; the noises and aromas, magically reconstructed; and the whole tinted with nostalgia.

These were tales of an endless array of journeys around our magical sea, starting with the rovings of that accident-prone King of Ithaka with Poseidon at his heel; of palaces reflected in shimmering waters, their eternal secrets carefully guarded behind intricate filigree-wood framed windows; of dazzling silks with an ethereal substance; of cool eastern gardens with reclining melancholic beauties in the foreground. For in our house, every painted cushion, every woven wall hanging, every kilim, every piece of silk, had a dazzling story to tell and these were told in unique fashion on long winter evenings.

To these, a number of people added the indispensable missing pieces, and the colourful puzzle was almost complete, but never finished. I am grateful to them all; to my friends Ange de Vena, Alicia Rios Ivars, Lala Isla, Vera Kyriakou, M. M. McKenzie with her Platonic 'entanglement', Manouella Pantazithou, Anna and Elias Psarrea, Dionysis Glykopantis, Kostas Goutis, Claudia Roden, Pepe Bosch, Guido Jesurum, Nevine Halici, Incilay Erendok, Aline Robinson, my cousin in Istanbul, Ivi Olgaç, my aunt Despina Patroni and my friend Sami Zubaida with whom the most argumentative sessions occur over the most sumptuous meals in his house. His arguments, like his food, are invaluable.

However, all these impressions and information would not have taken a form without the enthusiasm (and discipline) of my husband Graeme Salaman of whose passion for reading I have taken advantage on many occasions. He not only contributed unique information and sampled food and tradition around the Mediterranean ports with me, but also actively participated in my imaginary journeys around them, through my early impressions.

Also, I owe my gratitude to a multitude of people in markets and restaurants in various countries, not only for providing delicious food but also for patiently expounding on their cooking.

I am indebted to all the valuable books and sources that I consulted, particularly to the people who kindly allowed me to quote from them, and to those whom I took the liberty of quoting from anyway; in particular, Fernand Braudel's invaluable work on the Mediterranean, John Mavrokordatos and Chatto & Windus for Kavafi's *Ithaka*, the Islamic Culture Board for Professor Arberry's unique work, Mike and Tessa McKirdy of Cooks Books for Turabi Effendi, and Charles Perry for his fable-like articles on medieval Arab food.

For inspiration and encouragement I am grateful to Alan Davidson for his holistic approach to the Mediterranean in his *Mediterranean Seafood*, and to Elizabeth David, Jane Grigson and Claudia Roden for their eloquent style and enthusiasm on Mediterranean food. To John Lawton and Felicity Bryan of Curtis Brown for their support and encouragement. And, of course, my editor at Collins, Barbara Dixon, who brought order where before lay chaos, with patience and persistence.

RENA SALAMAN

RECIPE NOTES

Unless otherwise stated, all the recipes in this book will serve four people generously.

Quantities in the recipes are given in both metric and Imperial measures. Use either one or the other throughout the recipe, never both.

Oven Temperatures

The table below gives recommended equivalents:

	°C	°F	Gas Mark
Very cool	110	225	¼
	120	250	½
Cool	140	275	1
	150	300	2
Moderate	160	325	3
	180	350	4
Moderately hot	190	375	5
	200	400	6
Hot	220	425	7
	230	450	8
Very hot	240	475	9

Spoon measures

BRITISH	AMERICAN	AUSTRALIAN
1 teaspoon	1 teaspoon	1 teaspoon
1 tablespoon	1 tablespoon	1 tablespoon
2 tablespoons	3 tablespoons	2 tablespoons
3½ tablespoons	4 tablespoons	3 tablespoons
4 tablespoons	5 tablespoons	3½ tablespoons

All spoon measures given in the recipes are level unless otherwise stated.

A NOTE ON THE SELECTION
OF RECIPES

This book does not attempt to be an encyclopedic handbook of Mediterranean dishes. Probably no single volume could do that. While some recipes were thought too well known to need further publicity here, the criterion for selecting the recipes was that they should be quintessentially Mediterranean – steeped in 'Mediterraneanness'. The definition and analysis of this quality, which has preoccupied writers, artists and, more recently, tourists, is the essence of this book. The recipes, like the quality itself, are drawn from many sources and are the result of numerous different cultures, religions and influences. Paradoxically, from such variety, they are a celebration of gastronomic and spiritual unity – a casserole which surpasses its ingredients to achieve a distinct harmony.

INTRODUCTION

Kennst du das Land wo die Zitronen Bluhn?
Do you know the land where the lemon trees flower?
(*Mignonslied*, Goethe)

There is *one land*, or rather one sea, around which the lemon trees riot – the Mediterranean. It's France and Italy and Spain and Greece and Tunisia and Morocco and Egypt and Turkey, to mention just a few. All the countries around the Mediterranean seem to fuse into one image. They are the Mediterranean!

Is it possible that so many different countries with their distinct populations and cultures can be viewed as one? Arabs, Turks, Greeks and Latins, with their individual languages, religions and traditions, formed over the centuries a heterogeneous society around the shores of the Mediterranean, with vastly differing life styles, from idolatry to Christianity, with Jews and Muslims and Zoroastrians; mountain nomads and shepherds, plains farmers and island fishermen, urban labourers and skilled factory workers, seafarers and sailors; democrats and slaves, capitalists and communists.

How can we trace a sense of unity in this dense and composite human puzzle? It is because the peoples have been in constant and perpetual contact through conquering and colonizing, migrating and converting, trading and marrying. Also, as Fernand Braudel puts it, 'at the heart of this human unit ... there is a source of physical unity, a climate, which has imposed its uniformity on both landscape and ways of life ... that men and goods should be able to move from one to another without any need for acclimatization: such living identity implies the living unity of the sea. It is a great

15

deal more than a beautiful setting.' (*The Mediterranean and the Mediterranean World in the Age of Philip II.*)

It is this sea that has made the peoples of the Mediterranean uncompromising voyagers and adventurers. The mystique of the unknown beyond its blue expanse has had magnetic charm, difficult to cast aside. Indeed, it was Odysseus, King of Ithaka, with his mythical ten-year, homebound journey after the destruction of Troy, who made the oldest and most famous of all sea journeys!

Phoenicians and ancient Greeks colonized as far as Carthage and Marseilles respectively and it was these Greeks who are reputed to have introduced the first olive trees to Provence 2,500 years ago. Alexander and his Macedonian armies advanced to the East as far as India, where they first encountered rice and probably unfamiliar vegetables such as aubergines.

By the middle of the second century AD, as Greek power weakened, the Romans took over the entire Mediterranean and held it until AD 476 when the last Roman Emperor, Romulus Augustulus, was overpowered by the Barbarians. The Byzantines then, in their turn, controlled Sicily, Italy and North Africa. At the height of its power and prosperity, Byzantium was an Empire that spread from 'the Lebanon to the Danube and from Naples to the Caspian Sea', according to Steven Runciman in his *A History of the Crusades*. It was next the turn of the Arabs; their invasions of the seventh, eighth and ninth centuries, spreading the Koran from east to west, were an Arab equivalent of the Crusades. They also controlled, for a long time, North Africa, Spain and Sicily.

The Crusades followed – from the birth of the movement in the eleventh century to its decline in the fourteenth the whole of the eastern Mediterranean was conquered and occupied; and eventually it was the splendour and power of the Ottomans who conquered, advanced and occupied mainly east of the Sicilian straits while the Christians remained predominant in the West. History with all its splendour and of all sorts was made around the Mediterranean shores!

At a Commons debate once, an M.P. remarked, 'The people of Crete unfortunately make more history than they can consume locally'. The same remark could be applied to the whole of the Mediterranean.

It was through history that these diverse cultures intermingled, absorbed and at times fused. Spain, for instance, became totally Muslim, and during the tenth and eleventh centuries 'received all its cultural nourishment from the East, its poets, doctors, professors, philosophers, magicians and even its red-skirted dancers', according to Fernand Braudel. From these contacts an underlying sense of unity has been created, and this is particularly evident when it comes to culinary matters.

Mediterraneanness

The unity in diversity which is the characteristic feature of Mediterranean culture was achieved not only by mythical kings and colonizing armies, but by ordinary people travelling and trading in the course of everyday life: Levantine spice traders, Byzantine silk merchants, travelling buffoons, sailors – all contributed something from their respective cultures and ancestoral past. And in this lies the richness of Mediterranean culture; not a bland stew in which all the original ingredients have unrecognizably intermingled, but a rich *mélange* with an exoticism discernible to travellers and commentators over the centuries, achieved by the unique combination of persistently different ingredients.

Of course, there have been those who, coming from a radically different culture such as England, have noticed not the diversity of the Mediterranean countries but their exotic and homogeneous foreignness. Hilaire Belloc, for instance, expressed this accurately, if rather crudely, in his smug verse from *Ladies and Gentlemen*:

17

> The most degraded of them all
> Mediterranean we call.
> His hair is crisp and even curls
> And he is saucy with the girls.

Apart from the stereotyped appearance, and even sexual appetite, of the Mediterranean, there are other attributable characteristics, particularly concerning his emotional world; some a trifle exaggerated and others to the point. Mediterraneans are extrovert and sunny like their climate, hospitable, warm and immediate; but, above all, they are passionate about their likes as well as their dislikes. Theirs is an outdoor world, both physically and emotionally. Under the penetrating force of Mediterranean light there are left few dark corners in which to hide emotional skeletons. With their tendency for the extreme, everyday events are over-dramatized. Age-old market bargaining is an operatic event accompanied by appropriate facial expressions and gesticulating, even when it revolves round just a kilo of tomatoes. When it comes to political discussion the performance ranges from a saraband to an ancient Greek tragedy. The olive tree does not only constitute a geographical frontier between north and south but also an emotional one. Inwardness and repression do not flourish where the olive trees grow.

People have seen the Mediterranean temperament as representing a desirable, emotional wholeness; a triumph of Dionysius over Apollo. This view has always appealed to writers, both E. M. Forster and Germaine Greer celebrating, in rather different ways, the appeal of Tuscan lovers. Norman Douglas is quite clear on this theme of the emotionally impoverished Northerner, suffering inwardly, in contrast to the extravagantly expressive Mediterranean.

> Man alone is a perennial drudge. Yet many of us
> would do well to *mediterraneanise* ourselves for a season,
> to quicken those ethic roots from which has sprung
> so much of what is best in our own natures. To dream

18

is *Siren Land*, pursuing the moods, the memories as they shift in labyrinthine mazes, like shadows on a woodland path in June; to stroll among the hills and fill the mind with new images upon which to browse and leisure, casting off outworn weeds of thought with the painless ease of a serpent and unperplexing, incidentally, some of those 'questions of the day' of which the daily papers nevertheless know nothing – this is an antidote of many ills. (*Siren Land*.)

One of the best and most accurate usages of the adjective 'Mediterranean', is when it describes the explosion of colours of the region. However, Mediterranean colour does not simply bring to mind brilliant brushstrokes of different hues, it means much more! It implies the diffused purples of the minute flowers of wild thyme in the hills of Provence and the lavender flowers crowning Grasse in the Côte D'Azur; the sumptuous purples of a boatload of aubergines in the Venetian lagoons, and the pinks of Roman strawberries on a May morning. It is the imperial scarlets of roses in a luscious garden in Algiers, and the reds of the pomegranates exploding with ripeness among the autumnal colours; the rich saffron of Andalusian oranges and the crystalline yellows of the candied apricots and melons of Avignon.

It tantalizes the memory with evocations of the young green of pregnant figs, still garlanded with morning dew, in Smyrna; and for me it implies the bashful greens of lorry-loads of young artichokes, on their way to the Athenian markets from Peloponnisos. Also, the browns and coppers of the sun-cracked Tunisian earth; the whiteness of the dazzling almond blossoms in the crisp February air; and, best of all, the virginal creaminess of the lemon blossoms in May, at the hour of sunset in an Aegean island. All these are rendered more brilliant by the unique Mediterranean light which transforms even a stark and humble landscape. These and many more are the hues of the Mediterranean.

Apart from colour and light, there are other distinctive Mediterranean symbols. There are the cubic forms of brilliantly white-washed Aegean houses, which look as

19

though arranged by childish hands; and on the African coast, the sun-baked mud houses clinging to the earth which is always speckled with skinny domestic animals. Also, the pat-pat of the beaded doorway curtains, trembling under the breeze or melting under the midday sun, obstructing the heat and winged intruders from fragmenting the dark, cool peace of the inner sanctum sanctorum that every Mediterranean household possesses. Then there are the rows of dark and slender cypresses that stud the landscape, implanting a quality of peace and tranquillity on it; these are very often planted for practical purposes as a wall of protection against the temperamental north and north-easterly winds, the French *mistral*, the Spanish *tramontana*, the Italian *bora* and the Greek *meltemi*.

The Sea

Of course, the most Mediterranean of all symbols is the Sea itself, whose numerous charms contribute to the intricate patterns that comprise the fabled puzzle of the area. Even to the present day when pollution has become her major enemy, the Mediterranean retains her glittering spell, reflecting and exhausting the colours of the sky in the shimmering waters beneath. Sea and sky are interlocked in perpetual flirtation, like lovers reflected in each other's eyes.

In practical terms, the Mediterranean is not even one sea but is made up of different ones, such as the Adriatic, the Ionian, the Aegean, the Ligurian and the Tyrrhenian (Corsica and Sardinia). She is not a deep sea and her continental shelves (shallow areas near the land that make good fishing ground) are too narrow for the marine life to flourish. Also, according to oceanographers, the Mediterranean's waters are biologically exhausted because the sea is geologically too old.

Her main flow of life comes from the Atlantic waters which enter through the Straits of Gibraltar, and also from the Black Sea through the Sea of Marmara. Despite these, however, the Mediterranean is poor in plankton, which is the most important food factor for fish in the larval state, as Alan Davidson explains in his classic *Mediterranean Seafood*. Plankton can often be seen at night, a phosphorous, silvery ribbon appearing and disappearing on the surface of the seas like the jewel-studded tail of a mermaid dancing beneath. Alan Davidson says that even 'the famous blueness of the Mediterranean and the clarity of its waters portray this poverty.' I wonder, if Shelley and Byron had known about this, would they have reacted differently in their verses?

Nevertheless, poor in plankton or not, elderly or not, and perhaps even biologically exhausted as scientists claim, the Mediterranean still displays her famous blueness and the clarity of her waters is unmatched. Shelley sang about this same blueness in his *Ode to the West Wind*:

> Thou who didst waken from his summer dreams
> The blue Mediterranean, where he lay,
> Lulled by the coil of his crystalline streams
> Beside a pumice isle in Baiae's bay ...

And so, on this high note we disembark and explore the urban, cosmopolitan ports, bustling with energy and noise.

The Ports

The Mediterranean is a rich, inexhaustible source of symbols and images. Does it matter that some of these are simplistic or inaccurate? Like Kavafi's *Ithaka*, it is not the reality, but our dreams which matter; who cares what *Ithaka* is really like?

... You must pray that the way be long;
Many be the summer mornings
When with what pleasure, with what delight
You enter harbours never seen before;
At Phoenician trading stations you must stop,
And must acquire merchandise,
Mother of pearl and coral, amber and ebony,
And sensuous perfumes of every kind;
As much as you can get of sensuous perfumes;
You must go to many cities of Egypt,
To learn and still to learn from those who know.
... Ithaka has given you your lovely journey
Without Ithaka you would not have set out.
Ithaka has no more to give you now.

Poor though you find it, Ithaka has not cheated you.
Wise as you have become, with all your experience,
You will have understood the meaning of an Ithaka.

Like Kavafi's poem, we will embark on a journey round the
Mediterranean, stopping at Phoenician trading stations and
mythical ports, loaded with exoticism, such as Smyrna, where
my grandmother lived, or Istanbul where my mother came
from and which left such a strong haunting impression of
Orientalism on my childhood. Decaying, cosmopolitan
Alexandria, Kavafi's very own city and best seen through
his eyes; Piraeus, bustling with life and huge freighters,
which holds my most intimate childhood memories;
Thessaloniki on the Crusaders' route to the East, both by
land and by sea; Kyrenia and Canea, Sicily and Naples, Venice
and Marseilles, Algiers and Barcelona.

If mixture and diversity are the essence of *Mediterraneanness*,
then it is in these ports of the Mediterranean that this essence
is to be found; not only of the culture but of the characteristic
Mediterranean sights, sounds and smells.

Our arrival in these ports will also be a celebration; and we will fill with homesickness at the hot, nutty, sesame smell of the crusty rings of the wandering *simitçi* in the jewelled opulence and glittering gold of the Kapali Çarci – the covered market – in Istanbul. In the cobbled, hilly streets of Pera, its suburb, drawn by the throaty cries of the wandering *dondurmaçi*, we shall indulge in the creamy richness of his wares – a brilliantly white ice cream called *dondourma* – perfumed with the scent of the eastern vanilla pod. We shall quench our midday thirst on a hot April day, on the seafront in the Beirut of the 1960s, out of a little glass held by an aluminium ring, filled in rotation by the moustachioed Lebanese sherbet-seller, from glass jars glittering with the colours of fruit sherbets, strawberry with bright pink, orange with a vibrant saffron, and lemon with an astoundingly fresh green.

At sunset we will serenely sail into the medieval port of Chanea – Hania – in Crete, and sip thimblefuls of ouzo and taste the flavour of the sea from a plate of studded sea urchins. In Alexandria, in the early evening, we shall become drenched in the sensuous spiciness of the dark cummin seeds from the corner sellers' sizzling pots of the astounding *tamia* (*falafel*).

Next morning, in the Suq of Algiers, we shall stop for a sweetened mint tea out of a fragile china cup held by an ornate brass base; and at the hour of noon we shall enter a bar in Barcelona through its colourful beaded entrance and indulge and *Mediterraneanise* ourselves in the aroma of the frying garlic of the multiple *tapas* displayed for us. At the languid hour of the siesta, near the Rialto market in Venice, we shall feast our emotions in the scarlet explosion of Veronesean colour in an outsized, half-moon-shaped slice of the ripest of watermelons, studded with glittering sugary tears. And so, imperially refreshed, we are ready to journey inland over the fragrant hills and through the labyrinth of clustered villages.

The Mediterranean, A Frugal Tradition

> May God save you from the plague coming down
> from Castille and the famine coming up from
> Andalusia.

So Guzman de Alfarache is told in Mateo Aleman's *Vida del picaro Guzman de Alfarache*, in 1603.

In 1521 there was famine in Castille, and in Portugal the year was known as that of 'The Great Hunger'. In 1525 Andalusia was devastated by a terrible drought. In 1528 famine brought terror to Tuscany: Florence had to close her gates to the starving peasants from surrounding districts.

The bewitching explosion of multicoloured fruit and vegetables all around the Mediterranean creates an image of abundance, and perhaps affluence, which is false. The charming spell of light and colour plays a sorcerer's trick with our senses. There is a fair amount of rain and a more than fair amount of heat; but unfortunately they do not coincide. Drought has always been the plague of the Mediterranean peasant but at least now that imports of grain have become a certainty, Mediterranean life is not threatened at its roots with famine and death, as it was in the fifteenth and sixteenth centuries, or with poverty and destitution as in the eighteenth and nineteenth centuries.

Land suitable for cultivation is not abundant, as the Mediterranean terrain is rocky and full of lime, and stony hills have to be terraced before cultivation. The marbly grey or pink stones extracted are then used to build the satisfying dry walls that are to be found everywhere and which prevent the earth from disappearing like a torrential river with the next autumnal rains. Land is cultivated in rotation so that two or three different crops can be obtained. Richard Ford vividly describes a similar impression of Spain in 1848, in his *Gatherings from Spain*.

> ... It was a saying of the Grand Conde, 'If you want
> to know what want is, carry on a war in Spain.' ...All

who ride or run through the Peninsular, will read thirst in the arid plains, and hunger in the soil-denuded hills, where those who ask for bread will receive stones. The knife and fork question has troubled every warrior in Spain, from Henry IV down to Wellington: 'subsistence is the great difficulty always found' is the text of a third of the Duke's wonderful dispatches. This scarcity of food is implied in the very name of Spain, Σπάνια, which means poverty and destitution.

However, by the middle of the nineteenth century the situation had improved; bread was to be had, even if it was 'hard and black, even a year old and all of rye', the sort of bread that had to be cut with an axe. It was said that one was not considered a man until he had managed to cut his own stale bread. This bread, badly leavened, badly kneaded and prone to mould, black and indigestible, was still an 'object of veneration, never cut into until the sign of the cross was carved on it with a knife; and the sharing of bread was the very essence of companionship.' (Eugen Weber, *Peasants into Frenchmen*.)

A loaf of bread would always be crossed with a knife, by my grandmother in our household in Greece, before it was cut, and Greek peasants still perform the same ritual on a pristine loaf of bread. I recall that if the last morsel of bread was left at the table we were told that our strength was left behind and made to finish it. If a small piece of bread was accidentally dropped on the floor, there was a whole performance we had been taught to follow: picking it up, making the sign of the cross on it, kissing it and disposing of it in a very solemn manner in some quiet corner where no one would trample on it. Apparently in Spain they follow the same custom. Even to this day, when bread is unreverentially disposed of at the end of a meal I feel a pang of guilt about it.

In the nineteenth century, and in some Mediterranean countries in the twentieth too, bread was made from varied ingredients according to availability. Barley, rye, beans and carobs were all used and, during the famine of 1817 in the Maconnais, in France, the year of the great hailstorm, apparently nutshells were ground in an attempt to make bread.

However, even if bread was a luxury that people longed for, the bare minimum they survived on was a kind of soup. This might be gruel or porridge or any odd pieces of this and that boiled in water; in fact, for lack of anything else it was even just water and salt, with a little fat added if possible, for the peasants of France. Richard Ford gives a very similar image of Spanish diet in a somewhat extreme description '... a Peninsular breakfast [he says] consists of a teaspoonful of chocolate, a dinner of a knob of garlic soaked in water [the well known bread and garlic soup of Spain that has survived to the present day], and a supper of a paper cigarette; and according to their *parfait cuisinier* the *Olla* is made of two cigars boiled in three gallons of water – but this is a calumny, a mere invention devised by the enemy.' (The *Olla* being a kind of stew with a handful of varied ingredients, almost anything available, being simmered in an earthenware pot, for hours or overnight.) Chickpeas are indispensable for a true *Olla* and Richard Ford goes on to say: 'These *Garbanzos* – chickpeas – are the vegetable, the potato of the land.' Later, describing the *Olla* in practical terms, he concludes: 'In fact, as a general rule, anything that is good in itself is good for an *Olla* provided, as old Spanish books always conclude, that it contains nothing contrary to the Holy Mother church, to orthodoxy, and to good manners – "*que no contiene cosa que se oponga a nuestra madre Iglesia, y santa fe catolica, y buenas costumbres*".'

One of the most indicative signs of Mediterranean frugality is an incident which took place in the sixteenth century. The Grand Duke of Tuscany, when made liable by Philip II for supplying food for the Spanish and German soldiers crossing from Italy into Spain, kept the scarce quantities of salt meat for the German soldiers. Even though the Spaniards had arrived first, he knew that they would be content with rice and biscuits and would not raise an uproar. (Felipe Ruiz Martin, *Lettres marchandes échangées entre Florence et Medina del Campo.*)

Mediterranean diet was consequently shaped by natural habitat and circumstances and it has remained traditionally lighter and, by the nature of its ingredients, healthier than its northern European counterpart.

Religious and Social Taboos

At Brignolles, where we dined, I was obliged to quarrel with the landlady, and threaten to leave her house, before she would indulge us with any sort of fleshmeat. It was a meagre day, and she had made her provisions accordingly. She even hinted some dissatisfaction at having heretics in her house. But, as I was not disposed to eat stinking fish, with ragouts of eggs and onions I insisted upon a leg of mutton, and a brace of fine partridges, which I found in the larder. (Tobias Smollet, *Travels through France and Italy.*)

(I imagine the 'stinking fish' to have been salted cod!)

In addition to all the factors mentioned so far that have given Mediterranean diet its traditional pattern, a most important one is that of cultural and religious taboos. Muslims and Jews would not touch pork on the ritual grounds of its uncleanliness and this limited their dietary scope; and apart from this they observed strict fasting during Ramadan and Passover respectively. Christians, on the other hand, both Catholics as well as Orthodox, were also governed by long periods of religious fasting, the longest being the Easter

27

Lent lasting forty days, during which no animal products were permitted. A cathartic period, physically as well as spiritually.

In France these days of fast, which have been calculated at about one hundred and sixty-six including Lent, were observed so strictly until the reign of Louis XIV, in the seventeenth century, that meat of any kind or eggs etc., were forbidden for sale during the period of Lent except to invalids, who apparently needed for this purpose two certificates, one from the priest and the other from a doctor. The exceptional term of a 'Lent Butcher' of the time also indicates how seriously matters were taken. As a result, fish was in great demand, either fresh, salted or smoked. Moreover, on Wednesdays and Fridays throughout the year, to symbolize the sorrow of the same days which had seen Christ tried and crucified, Christians would not touch any animal products. This was so strictly observed in Byzantine times that during the reign of Leon the Wise (886–912) in Constantinople, a most prosperous city at the time, the sale of meat was entirely forbidden on such days by Royal decree. Boiled beans of all kinds, including chickpeas and lentils, dressed with freshly grated nutmeg, were eaten instead by the fasting Byzantines. Indeed, the Byzantine Church, with its highly ascetic image and accent on monasticism, criticized the consumption of meat as unhealthy for body and mind, in a general cloud of disapproval.

Indicative of the strong trend of fasting traditions on Wednesdays and Fridays is an incident that occurred in 1185 when the Normans took Thessaloniki. The massacre of the population and pillaging that followed have been described movingly and in horrifying detail by the Archbishop of the time, Efstathios. However, as if this was not enough, and in yet another outburst of vengeance, during Lent the Normans deliberately mixed animal fat into the olive oil for sale, in order to contaminate the fasting populace, which caused an uproar. This fasting pattern of diet is still observed in most Mediterranean countries, perhaps not so much governed by religious fervour any more, as much as by habit.

In France, Italy, Greece and Spain one finds fish on restaurant menus on Fridays including salted cod, as in the Middle Ages.

Such was the religious climate that helped to shape Mediterranean diet into its traditional form and give it a uniquely constant pattern through the ages.

The Olive

If Homer were to take a look at the Mediterranean today, he would be astounded by the trees and produce we think of as being typically Mediterranean: orange, lemon, mandarin and peach trees from Indochina, cypresses from Persia, eucalyptus trees from Australia, watermelons from Africa, and all those American natives that have become indispensable in Mediterranean cooking since they were introduced to Europe by the Spaniards and the Portuguese in the fifteenth century – potatoes, beans, maize, peppers and tomatoes.

Despite these, the most dominantly Mediterranean of trees is the gnarled but always beautiful olive tree, indigenous in its wild form in the eastern Mediterranean. It was probably cultivated in Syria as early as 6000 BC. *Olea Europea* derives its name from the ancient Greek *Elaia*, and according to mythology it was created by the goddess Athena in her strife with Poseidon over the patronage of the city of Athens. It was cultivated in Minoan Crete since Neolithic times, but it was particularly encouraged and funded and so became widely cultivated in Classical Greece; olive groves are mentioned by Homer, and olive oil was exported from Attica before and during the time of the Athenian legislator, Solon (638–559 BC). It was from the eastern Mediterranean shores that the olive tree, together with its illustrious native companion, the vine, travelled westwards, following the course of history with the colonizing Greeks as far as Spain and Provence. And while today one automatically thinks of Spain, Italy, France and perhaps Greece as the main olive oil producers, the African Mediterranean coast has also been a good source in the past; Tunisia had flourishing olive groves during Roman times and the island of Djerba, off the south Tunisian coast, was a prolific producer during the sixteenth century. Indeed, at the end of the sixteenth century, it was to Djerba that the English turned for their imports of olive oil which, up to then, had been supplied by Spain.

And in the early nineteenth century an Italian traveller in the area commented on the growth of olive trees and vines thus:

> Vines grow to a prodigious height, and passing naturally from one tree to another, form beautiful arbours; their size is equally remarkable, being sometimes as large at the root as a tolerably proportioned olive tree. The latter is also a very favourite production of northern Africa; and besides the immense quantities of trees, wild and cultivated, the Algerine territory produces a small thorny tree, which bears a fruit equal in size and flavour to the large olive of Spain. (Signor Pananti, *Narrative of a Residence in Algiers.*)

The sharp and pungent fruit of the olive tree are undoubtedly the protagonists of Mediterranean diet and appear splendidly undisputed on frugal or regal tables, often made into appetizers such as the sharp, creamy Provençal *tapenade*, a blend of capers and anchovies, derived from the ancient Provençal word *tapeno* which means capers; in Turkey, a spoon preserve is made with them; they appear cooked in colourful ragouts, particularly in Morocco, France, Greece and Spain; and even in lovely hot crusted bread that is made on the island of Cyprus and appropriately called *eliopitta*.

When pressed, the olive renders the most important and most precious of liquids in the area, the olive oil. It is olive oil that has particularly shaped the cuisine of the area and given it its distinctive flavour and identity, especially so in vegetable cooking. In World War Two, during the German occupation in Greece, olive oil became the most precious commodity in a world of bartering and black-marketeers who recognized its potential value, manipulated its marketing and consequently made fortunes from it.

Social status was often critically decided according to the amount of olive oil that a vegetable dish contained; a few of the familiar watery bubbles intercepting an already thin sauce could mean a family tumbled down the social ladder instantly. A thick, oily and rich sauce, on the other hand, meant affluence and prosperity.

According to Maximilien Sorre in his article *Les Fondements Biologiques de la Géographie Humaine*, published in 1943: 'One of the peculiarities of the peoples who lived on the periphery of the Mediterranean world, which most astonished the Ancients, was the use of cows' butter: those accustomed to olive oil viewed this with shocked surprise. Even an Italian like Pliny had the same reaction, forgetting that after all the use of olive oil had not been established in Italy for so very long.'

> Because of the butter and dairy produce which is so widely used in Flanders and Germany, these countries are overrun with lepers. (Fernand Braudel)

Thus exclaimed the Cardinal of Aragon on reaching the Netherlands in 1517 with his cook and his own supplies of olive oil.

In a typically Mediterranean outburst, the Cardinal of Aragon was exaggerating a little of course! And if nowadays, northern countries, where excessive use of butter and dairy products have been predominant in the daily diet, are not 'overrun with lepers', they are overrun with heart disease and other circulatory disorders. Modern medical research attributes these, to a great extent, to products rich in cholesterol.

Olive oil, which contains no cholesterol, is a mono-unsaturated fat which has been proved to possess major beneficial qualities over other oils and fats. It not only reduces the amounts of LDL (low-density lipoprotein) in the blood, the harmful cholesterol that encourages fat deposits in the arteries, but at the same time it leaves untouched HDL (high-density lipoprotein), which helps to eliminate cholesterol from the blood. Polyunsaturated oils, on the other hand, tend to lower both LDL and HDL, and while the first is beneficial the second is not.

Mediterranean peasants still regard olive oil as a remedy for all; and in a confidently instinctive manner they have always believed that olive oil not only enhances their diet, but certainly prolongs their life span as well, like that of the olive tree, which is reputed to be eternal!

The Dishes and their Historical Continuity

In the sixteenth century, a native of the Mediterranean, wherever he might come from, would never feel out of place in any part of the sea. To later colonial settlers their journey simply meant finding in a new place the same trees and plants, the same food on the table that they had known in their homeland; it meant living under the same sky, watching the same familiar seasons. (Fernand Braudel)

What was true in sixteenth-century Mediterranean countries is also true today, although perhaps not to the same extent, as differing levels of industrialization have made some countries more affluent than others. However, the Mediterranean's basic food pattern retains its strong links with the past.

The Middle Eastern *tarator* or Greek *skorthalia*, the Italian *agliata*, basically all garlic-based sauces thickened with bread, almonds or walnuts, are the same as *skorothalmi*, a favourite of ancient Athenians. (Aspasia Miha-Lambaki, *The Diet of the ancient Greeks according to the ancient playwrights*.) When diluted with water, it even becomes a soup, the Andalusian *gazpacho blanco*. And when thickened with eggs it became the French *aïoli* and Spanish *ali oli*. Do we owe this sharp appetizing sauce to the ancient Athenians or is there yet another source buried in the more distant past?

Pasta of a multitude of shapes is still at the heart of each Italian meal (as it was in the days of Boccaccio, 1313–75), and despite the delicate flavour of the veal dishes that may follow as *I Secondi*, a plate of beans will still be found on most Italian tables. The Spaniards still love their *garbanzos* and their *tortillas*. The Greeks still eat their lentils, beans and chickpea soups on Wednesdays and Fridays, and in Turkey chickpeas are found in most soups and in pilafs with rice or cracked wheat. The Arabs cook pulses with vegetables, with poultry and meat and they make the best of them in a wealth of ways. The great tradition of pulses is shared throughout the Mediterranean. Chickpeas in soups such as the Italian *minestra di ceci*, the French *soupe aux pois chiches* from Languedoc, the Greek *revithia soupa*, the Spanish *garbanzos salteados*, or the Turkish *nohut çorbasi* are nourishing, healthy and absolutely delicious. In the Middle East, puréed with olive oil, garlic, tahina and cummin, they create the enticing *humus*.

As for beans, they are everywhere! Beans of every shape, size and hue; *cannellini*, haricot, the marbled red-and-beige *borlotti* beans, various butter beans or lima beans, the broad beans etc. Treated in a multitude of ways, they make soups, casseroles and salads. All in all, the Mediterranean must be the bean belt of the world.

Apart from the continuity that is to be found within the individual diet of each country, there is an astonishing wealth of similarities in the various cuisines, not only in the ingredients, which could easily be attributed to the identical rural economies, but also in the dishes, though with an idiosyncratic touch from one country to another. These can

33

be ascribed to the shared historical influences and background of the area.

The origin of dishes can be traced step by step to some very unexpected sources. A number of dishes in Spain, and even France and Italy, stem from the Arab tradition through the Moorish conquests that held parts of the Iberian Peninsular and Sicily for as long as eight hundred years. For instance, a delicious concoction of fried spinach with raisins and pine kernels, known in Spain as *espinacas a la Catalana*, and in Italy as *spinaci alla Romana*, is identical to similiar dishes in the Arab countries.

Waverley Root, however, in his book *The Food of France*, casts doubt on such influences, perhaps in an over-generalizing way: 'Actually there is nothing particularly exotic about the cooking of the Arabs of North Africa, while in the Near and Middle East whatever unusual influences have crept into the menu are not Aabic in origin but come from non-Arabic Muslims – for instance, the Turks, who themselves though not immune to ideas arriving from Persia or India, owed a great deal to the Greeks, which gets us back again to the European shores of the Mediterranean.'

One wonders then, if such dishes as *espinacas a la Catalana* were adopted by the Moors, through the Arab invasions, from an original Persian tradition, rich at any rate in pine nuts and raisins. Or, as such ingredients were favoured by the Byzantines as standard fare for their stuffings, could the source of this dish be elsewhere, as Waverly Root suggests? Furthermore, could there have been an influence on the Byzantines by the Persians or vice versa?

As the Persian culinary tradition was full of splendour and a catalyst of the mystical intensities of the East in exquisite balances of sweet and sour, of dishes combining fruit with meat, nuts, vegetables and spices, it is possible that the influence spread to the Byzantine culinary tradition also. With a religion such as Zoroastrianism, in pre-Islamic Persia, where one of its main points was on active enjoyment of this world, experiencing life to the full as opposed to the asceticism of Christianity, one might understand their rich and elaborate culinary tradition. The splendid banquets of the Persians were not rejected as worldly; on the contrary one could say that they were prescribed by their religion! Such an opposing culture, at least on this one aspect of life, might have exercised a certain fascination on the abstemious Byzantines.

If that was the case, the Persian culinary influences would have found their way not only through the Arab invasions of the seventh, eighth and ninth centuries to Morocco, Spain and Sicily, but also through the traders who visited the heart of Byzantium, Constantinople, and brought back to their own countries, not only her exquisite wares but also stories of splendour and mysticism, of golden palaces and treasures, of exquisite banquets with new dishes and spices:

> Constantinople had never before been so wealthy. It was the unrivalled financial and commercial capital of the world. Traders from far and wide, from Italy and Germany, from Russia, from Egypt and the East, came crowding there to buy the luxuries produced by its factories and to exchange their own *rougher wares*. The bustling life of the vast city, far more extensive and populous than even Cairo or Baghdad, never failed to amaze the traveller with its crowded harbour, its full bazaars, its wide suburbs and its tremendous churches and palaces. (Steven Runciman)

Sweet and sour dishes, for instance, originated in ancient, pre-Islamic, Zoroastrian Persia during the Sassanid period and would have been brought to Morocco through the various invasions. This is obviously the route by which they found their way to Spain, particularly in Catalonian cooking, and Sicily. These dishes, known as ... *all agrodulce*, which could be vegetables or meat in a thick sauce of vinegar and sugar, could also contain a little grated chocolate, which would have been a later influence, imported by the Spaniards in about 1520, during the reign of Philip II, from Mexico.

The Dishes

The Basque dish *pipérade*, an omelette with fresh tomatoes and sweet peppers, known as *chakchouka* in Tunisia, has come full circle around the Mediterranean; it is eaten by Turks, Greeks, Italians, Arabs and French with the same vigour and minor variations.

The simplest snack throughout the Mediterranean is a hefty slice of bread, rubbed with a sliced clove of garlic, then with a sliced tomato and finally a generous sprinkling of olive oil and perhaps a little wild marjoram. This is the Spanish *el-pa-y-all*, the Maltese *hobz biz zejt*, the Greek *riganatha*; it is also eaten by the French and the Turks. And in Andalusia there is a local variation in which the bread is soaked in the juice of half an orange, then sprinkled with olive oil and finally spread with honey; this is called *pan con zumo de naranja, aceite de oliva y miel*. When we were children, during the winter months when tomatoes were not available, we had a variation of this bread with olive oil concoction, to which we were addicted; the bread was covered with a thin layer of tomato paste (home-made in those days) with the olive oil on top; I believe this was also common in the Middle East. I still cannot decide which had the most dramatic effect on us – its sharp, engulfing taste or the mystique surrounding the ritual.

Throughout the recipes, the similarities in dishes of various countries have been indicated in order to demonstrate to the reader this 'holistic' approach to Mediterranean food.

APPETIZERS
(Mezze, Antipasti, Tapas),
PIES, PICKLES
AND SAUCES

Appetizers

After Pastry of *Tardina*
Follows *Sanbusaj*, well fried;
Eggs vermillioned after boiling
Lie with olives side by side.

Strips of tender meat in slices,
Dipped in oil of finest make,
Tempt anew the flagging palate
And the appetite awake;

Lemons, too, with *Nadd* besprinkled
Scented well with ambergris,
And, for garnishing the slices,
Shreds of appetising cheese.

Vinegar that smarts the nostrils
Till they snuffle and they run;
Little dates like pearls, that glisten
On a necklace one by one.

Sauce of *Buran* served with egg-plant
That will tempt thy very heart,
And asparagus – enchanted
With asparagus thou art!

Lastly, *Lozenge*, soaked in butter,
Buried deep in sugar sweet.
And a saki's cloven dimples
Promise joy when lovers meet.

Mahmud ibn al-Husain al-Kushajim, who was a poet, astrologer and culinary expert in the service of the Hamsanid ruler Saif al-Daula, apparently described a favourite feast in the above evocative way. ('A Baghdad cookery book', a thirteenth-century manuscript, translated by Professor A. J. Arberry in *The Islamic Culture*.)

Herodotus, on the other hand, tells us that the Egyptians built the Great Pyramid on a diet of onions, bread and radishes. And Aristophanes, in his *Women in Government*, tells us that part of the soldiers' basic rations carried in their knapsacks, was 'bread, two onions and olives'.

Even nowadays, the peasant working on his land or the worker in the factory, Arab, Turk, Greek or Spaniard, will untie a colourful napkin, under the shade of a tree, to unveil his simple lunch: a quartered onion, a hard piece of home-made bread, with an enticing, sharply sour taste, a few shiny olives and that vivacious American newcomer to the Mediterranean, the scarlet tomato; all in all, not dissimilar to the lunch enjoyed by the ancient labourers beavering away at the pyramids, or the marching Greek soldiers.

With the last rays of the sun waning, the same peasant, sitting in the tranquillity of his white-washed courtyard, surrounded by pots of aromatic, clove-scented carnations, or on the chipped marble edge of a dry, decaying fountain, or under a palm tree surrounded by the ochre folds of the immense desert, expects something sharper, grander and richer to satisfy his palate and feed his imagination.

Perhaps not a feast such as that described by al-Kushajim, who was obviously relaying some courtly event, but nevertheless some of those same dishes that have been enjoyed for centuries and are still eaten today. All kinds of little pies, from the medieval Arab *sanbusak* to the similar present-day Turkish *börek* (page 64), have been part of the *mezze* table throughout the Eastern Mediterranean since time immemorial – indeed cheese pies were served at the tables of the ancient Greeks, under the name of *plakountes* or *tyroplakountes*. Occasionally large, but more often miniature, these pies harbour a thousand and one secrets, like the

40

sparkling pieces of an exploding star, captured and enwrapped firmly by the crisp layers of feather-like *fyllo* pastry; an Ali-Baba's cave! The gems may include nuts of all kinds, grainy rice, spinach, soft, crumbly sheep's cheese, raisins, eggs, minced meat or chicken, the warm spices of the East, or the fragrance of the hillsides of the West.

Sauce of Buran (fabled to have been served at the illustrious event of Buran's wedding, see page 111) was probably not very different from the enticing aubergine purée with tahina, known throughout the Arab world as *baba ghanoush*, in Turkey as *patlican kebab*, or *melitzanosalata* in Greece.

Pickles of all kinds, cauliflower, chillies, carrots, cucumbers, grapes, aubergines, etc. are very popular as part of the *mezze* all over the Mediterranean. Tiny aubergines, the early yield of the summer, are filled with cloves of garlic and tied with strings of celery, then freshly pickled with 'vinegar that smarts the nostrils till they snuffle and they run'. (See the medieval Arab recipe of *badhinjan mukhallal* and the Turkish *badingan turshussu* by Turabi Effendi, page 76.)

Then there are the dips and the purées; from the East, *skorthalia* or *caçik* with fried vegetables; the revitalizing spiced *humus*, made with a purée of chickpeas; *tahinosalata*, *taramosalata* and *tarator*; and in the west, *tapenade*, *anchoïade*, *bagna cauda*, *aïoli*, etc.

Another popular appetizer are the glorious little 'parcels' – the dark green leaves of the ubiquitous vines, or the orange-edged fragile courgette flowers, with rice, sweet onions and fragrant herbs nestling in them.

All in all, the *mezze* table is a precious mosaic combining the glorious colours of the Mediterranean, its tastes and its inexhaustible aromas.

Tapénade

Tapénade, which derives its name from the ancient Provençal word *tapéno* – capers – is a thick paste, served, almost in the same way as butter, in small, mustard-coloured, glazed, earthenware pots, the kind which are so common in France in all shapes and sizes.

It can be part of a platter of cold hors d'oeuvres and is almost always accompanied by sliced, hard-boiled eggs. Alternatively, you can slice hard-boiled eggs in two lengthways, remove the yolks, mix them with the *tapénade* and then fill the cavities of the eggs with the mixture. A little finely chopped tarragon or parsley is then sprinkled on top. Serve with a platter of crudités, including carrots, tender sticks of celery, raw artichoke hearts, cauliflower florets, pieces of young courgettes, different kinds of olives and delicious tiny slices of raw pickled or marinated fish, such as brill or salmon.

Tapénade combines the very basic Mediterranean ingredients: the fruit of the olive tree, aromatic golden lemons, the fruit of the wild growing, trailing caper plants with their exquisite lily-like, pink-petalled blossoms, and the anchovy, a common product of the Mediterranean. No doubt in the old days this was a good way to use up salted fish, which would have been kept pressed in earthenware jars, with thick sea salt spread between the layers, as families still do on the Greek islands, in Sicily and parts of Spain, for the winter months.

Collectively and independently, they are the same ingredients that have always been served routinely as very basic and unpretentious appetizers. However, from these basics the creation of *tapénade* was just one further step – to mix them all, with an alchemist's hand to achieve the right proportions.

Olives vary from region to region and from country to country. Some are smooth and velvety oily (I am referring solely to taste here and not to texture), while others can have layer on layer of flavours – from sweet to pungent to bitter. As a result, *tapénade* will vary in taste from time to time depending on what olives are used.

The concentration of flavours, strong and robust, and the texture of the dish give it a unique earthiness that seems to reflect the core of peasant life. Provençal or Mediterranean robustness could not be better expressed or represented in one dish.

    170g (6oz) stoned black olives, chopped roughly
    4 anchovy fillets
    85g (3oz) tuna fish
    2 tablespoons rinsed and drained capers
    1 clove garlic, peeled and chopped
    2 tablespoons lemon juice
    1 tablespoon brandy
    Freshly ground black pepper
    3—tablespoons olive oil

Place all the ingredients, except the olive oil, in a food processor or blender and mix to a smooth paste. With the machine still running, slowly add the olive oil.

Adjust the seasoning according to taste; perhaps a little more lemon juice or brandy, or a little more olive oil if you find the taste too strong, will be needed. I prefer to serve the *tapénade* at room temperature, unless we are in the middle of a very hot day in which case it tastes better slightly chilled.

Tahinosalata
A Tahina Dip

Tahina, or tahini, paste, made from crushed sesame seeds, is one of the most favourite ingredients in the Middle East. Combined with a few aromatic partners and diluted with lemon juice, it makes this dip a favourite dish all over the Middle East and Cyprus.

Serve *tahinosalata* as an appetizer with hot *pitta* or toast to dip into it, or as an accompaniment to almost any hot or cold vegetable dish, or with kebabs.

> 5 tablespoons tahina paste
> 150ml (5 fl oz) warm water
> 2 cloves garlic, peeled and chopped
> 1/4 teaspoon ground cummin (optional)
> Salt
> 4—5 tablespoons vegetable oil
> 5—6 tablespoons lemon juice
> 4—5 black olives to garnish

If the tahina paste in the jar looks separated from its oil, stir well with a spoon to mix. In a food processor or blender, blend the tahina, water, garlic, cummin and salt briefly, then, with the machine still running, slowly add the vegetable oil and lemon juice alternately. Blend until the mixture looks creamy in colour and texture. Adjust seasoning and serve garnished with the olives.

Caçik
Yoghurt Dip

Refreshing *caçik* is served with slices of fried aubergines or courgettes, or with *kebabs*. Often it is also offered with the formidable casseroles of fresh seasonal vegetables such as *bakla* – which contains fresh broad beans.

> 225g (8oz) plain yoghurt, preferably a thick sheep's one such as the Greek make Total or Delta
> 2 tablespoons olive oil
> 1 teaspoon vinegar
> 1 clove garlic, peeled and crushed
> Salt
> 10cm (4in) piece of cucumber, peeled and grated thickly
> 8 fresh mint leaves, finely chopped, *or* ½ teaspoon dried mint

In a bowl, beat together the first five ingredients. Add the cucumber and the mint. Stir well and serve chilled.

Anchoïade
Anchovy and Garlic Spread

A dish with all the qualities its name suggests, sharply appetizing, aromatic and satisfying. It is very similar, at least in content if not in the way it is served, to the Italian *bagna cauda*. Since it is difficult to find salted anchovies in barrels or cans in Britain, we have to use the canned variety, strained from their oil first. However, if salted ones are used, they should be properly rinsed and filleted. Skin and split each one down the middle lengthways, remove the central bone, soak the fillets in cold water for 10 minutes and rinse again.

Serves 4—6

2 × 45g (1½oz) cans of anchovy fillets, drained and chopped (7 fillets approximately per can)
2 cloves garlic, peeled and crushed
Freshly ground black pepper
¼ teaspoon dried thyme
5—6 tablespoons olive oil
2 tablespoons lemon juice
4 slices from a large loaf of bread, quartered or 3 celery sticks

Place the anchovies, garlic, pepper and thyme in a food processor or blender and blend into a rough paste. With the machine still running, slowly add the olive oil and lemon juice alternately until the mixture forms a creamy paste. Toast the bread and spread it with a thin layer of the *anchoïade*. Place under a hot grill briefly until lightly crisp and golden and serve immediately.

Alternatively, trim, wash and dry the celery and spread a thin layer of *anchoïade* into its cavity. Cut into bite-sized portions and serve cold.

Eliopitta or Elioti
Savoury Olive Bread

CYPRUS

Eliopitta is not simply a kind of bread but a meal in itself, full of sunny flavours and earthy tastes.

In fact, it is the combination of the two most basic items

eaten at all times throughout the Mediterranean: a piece of crusty bread and black olives. And since trouble has been taken to combine and knead these ingredients into something more appetizing and special, why not add some greenery from the hills or the garden in order to enhance the flavour and aroma? The result is indeed delicious.

Freshly baked, these crusty rolls are magnificent, cold they are unforgettably robust! They are excellent for a picnic and are also good offered with drinks before dinner. They can be frozen once baked, taken out and allowed to defrost for a couple of hours and then warmed in the oven.

I was introduced to these by my friend Vera Kyriakou and this is her recipe.

The following quantities will produce approximately 22 rolls and if this amount sounds enormous I can assure you they will be consumed very quickly.

450g (1lb) fresh spinach, trimmed
1 bunch fresh coriander, washed and drained
225g (8oz) onions or 2 bunches spring onions, trimmed
450g (1lb) oily olives, preferably stoned*
30g (1oz) fresh yeast
600ml (1 pint) warm water
1kg (2lb) plain or wholemeal flour, sifted
A little salt
150ml (5fl oz) olive oil

*Do not use sharp olives soaked in vinegar, such as the Greek Kalamata variety, but an oily, wrinkly kind.

Wash the spinach meticulously until no trace of grit remains, then drain it. Chop all the drained and prepared vegetables finely, including the onions. Stone the olives if necessary; they can be used with the stone in but do warn your guests before they eat the bread! If the olives are kept in brine they will be extremely salty and should be rinsed briefly before using.

Dissolve the yeast in 300ml (10fl oz) of the warm water.

Mix the flour, salt and olive oil together well. Add the dissolved yeast to the flour mixture, mix well and knead it with your knuckles for 10 minutes. Keep adding more of the remaining warm water as necessary. You may not need all of it but the dough should be quite wet and sticky.

In a separate bowl, mix all the chopped vegetables with the olives and a little salt. Add these to the dough, mix well and knead it again until all the greenery is well incorporated in the dough. Cover with a clean, thick tea towel and let it rest in a warm place for approximately 45 minutes, or until it is well risen.

Oil a baking tray with vegetable oil, and also oil your hands to prevent the dough from sticking. Divide the dough into pieces approximately 8cm (3in) in diameter and shape into round rolls; arrange on the baking tray. Keep oiling your hands while you are working.

Preheat the oven to gas no. 7 (425°F/220°C), place baking tray on the middle shelf and cook for 15 minutes, then turn the heat down to gas no. 5 (375°F/190°C) and cook for a further 15 minutes, until they are nicely brown.

Remove from oven and continue baking the rest of the rolls in the same way.

Tabbouleh
A Parsley Salad

LEBANON

Tabbouleh, with its strikingly rich tastes, layer upon layer of flavours contrasting with the aromatic freshness of the parsley, is much more than just a salad. It is to me, the 'Imperial' relative of the salad family. There cannot be a mezze table without the green-and-ochre platter of tabbouleh, strategically placed to delight the eye.

It was always part of the deliciously rich spread of mezze at the Commodore Hotel in Beirut where we used to stay overnight when on flights to Beirut. It makes the perfect match for *tamia* (page 39) and all kinds of *kebabs*.

> 85g (3oz) fine cracked wheat (*burghul*), picked clean
>   of stones
> 1 bunch flat-leafed continental parsley, if available,
>   trimmed, washed and drained, *or* use ordinary
>   parsley
> 1 medium onion, skinned and chopped finely
> 2 spring onions, trimmed
> 1 medium tomato, washed and diced
> 5cm (2in) piece of cucumber, diced
> 3 tablespoons fresh mint, chopped finely
> 6 tablespoons olive oil
> Juice of 1 lemon
> Salt and freshly ground black pepper

Soak the cracked wheat in warm water for 30 minutes; drain and squeeze it gently. Spread on a clean tea towel and roll up in order to dry it. Place the cracked wheat in a bowl, add all the remaining ingredients and toss gently. Spread on a flat platter and serve.

Baba Ghanoush
An Aubergine Salad

SYRIA/EGYPT/LEBANON

This enticing, smoky appetizer of aubergines, with all its variations, is popular in the eastern Mediterranean. *Melitzanosalata* to the Greeks, and *patlican kebabi* to the Turks, it is found throughout the Aegean basin. Ideally, the aubergines should be grilled slowly on charcoal in order to contribute that particular exotic, smoky flavour that identifies the dish. Since it is not always possible to embark on such outdoor activities, it is quite acceptable to roast the aubergines in the oven or under a grill, until they are properly cooked.

- 1kg (2lb) large aubergines
- 3 tablespoons tahina paste
- 2 tablespoons olive oil *or* vegetable oil
- Juice of 1½ lemons
- 3 cloves garlic, peeled and crushed
- 1 teaspoon ground cummin
- Salt and freshly ground black pepper
- 6—7 black olives to garnish

Prick the aubergines with a fork, place in a preheated oven, gas no. 4 (350°F/180°C), and cook for 1 hour, turning occasionally. When cool, scoop out the flesh, squeeze to extract any bitter juices and blend the flesh with the remaining ingredients until smooth. Taste and adjust seasoning. Serve on a platter with a few olives on top and hot *pittes* or fresh bread.

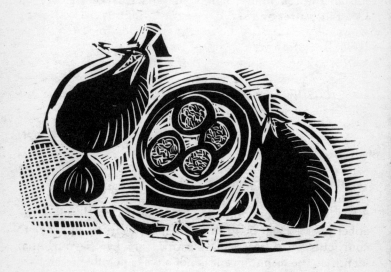

Zaalouk
Aubergine Salad

MOROCCO

This is a tasty dish which can be served hot or cold along with a rice dish and some fried fish, or as part of an array of appetizers. It is the recipe of Aline Robinson.

> 1kg (2lb) aubergines, trimmed, peeled and cubed in 2.5cm (1in) pieces
> 150ml (5fl oz) olive oil
> 5 cloves garlic, chopped finely
> 1½ teaspoons ground cummin
> ½ teaspoon cayenne pepper
> 1 teaspoon paprika
> 450g (1lb) tomatoes, peeled, de-seeded and chopped
> 3 tablespoons finely chopped fresh coriander or parsley
> Salt

Place the aubergines in a saucepan of lightly salted boiling water, bring back to the boil and simmer for 15 minutes. Drain and mash with a fork.

In a frying pan, heat the olive oil and sauté the garlic and spices briefly until aromatic, then add the tomatoes and cook for 10 minutes. Add the aubergines, the herbs, and some salt, mix and simmer uncovered until quite dry, about 15 minutes.

Humus Bi Tahina

Spicy Chickpea Salad

A trip to any of the Middle Eastern countries will also be an introduction to *humus* which is ubiquitous in those lands, served in a small and unpretentious *lokanta* around the Kapali Çarci in Istanbul, or from the *falafel* stalls of the bustling Cairo streets, or around the dark, labyrinth streets of the central market in Beirut where I first encountered it. It would arrive alongside tiny barbecued *poussins*, and even the jasmine-scented gardens around us at the Commodore Hotel would come alive with the pungent aroma of garlic.

Serve with fresh bread or *pitta*, to be dipped in it, or as a sauce with grilled chicken, or *kebabs*. It can be stored in the refrigerator for 3–4 days. Do not use canned chickpeas, as the result is very poor compared with the authentic dish.

Serves 6

**225g (8oz) chickpeas, picked clean, soaked
  overnight and rinsed
2 cloves garlic, peeled and chopped
2 tablespoons tahina paste
Juice of 1½ lemons
1½ teaspoons ground cummin
5 tablespoons vegetable oil
300ml (10fl oz) of the chickpea cooking liquid
Salt and freshly ground black pepper
1—2 tablespoons olive oil
A little cayenne pepper**

Place the chickpeas in a large saucepan with plenty of water, bring to the boil, and skim until clear. Cover and simmer for about 1 hour until soft. (In a pressure cooker it will only take 20 minutes.) Drain, reserving the cooking liquid. Add the remaining ingredients, except the olive oil and cayenne, to the chickpeas and divide the mixture into two.

Blend each batch briefly in a liquidizer. The mixture should be grainy and of a runny consistency, rather than smooth and pasty. Adjust seasoning and blend briefly. Serve on a flat platter, with the olive oil and the cayenne sprinkled decoratively on top.

Tamia or Falafel
Spicy Broad Bean Rissoles

EGYPT/ISRAEL

This is one of the best examples of 'how much can be made out of how little'. A great appetizer and a landmark in Arab cuisine. Tamia are best served hot with a colourful salad; they are also delicious with the Turkish *caçik* or *humus*, and, of course, together with any of the vegetable and pulse-casseroles they add spice to a meal.

In the mid-1960s, while I was flying with Olympic Airways, even though we used to stay in the rather illustrious surroundings of the historic Shepherds' Hotel in central Cairo, I could hardly wait to go down into the crowded and noisy streets and buy a paper funnel of *falafels* from the nearest seller. (I also bought several more to take back with me the following day, for my grandmother in Athens who was addicted to them!)

However, the most exciting event, always, was the visit to the *El Filfila* (The Chilli) restaurant, with its eccentric decoration of lively monkeys in cages. There, as you entered, with the cooking counters in full view, amidst the noise, the cooking aromas and smoke, you could see the frenzied activities of the cooks squeezing the *falafel* out through their hands; then the perfectly round walnut-sized balls would go into the bubbling hot oil of their cauldrons. And in turn you could sample the *falafel* – the best of all – golden, crisp, crunchy and spicy, enclosing all the secret flavours of the

53

earth within, accompanied by a bottle of what else but Ptolemy wine! (The alternative being a rather cheeky *Châteaux Giannaklis!*)

In Israel *falafel* are made with chickpeas but I prefer the Egyptian version with dried broad beans, or even a mixture of both. Skinned, dried broad beans can be bought in packets from Greek and other delicatessens.

Serves 6—8

225g (8oz) skinned, dried broad beans, cleaned and
   soaked for 24 hours
225g (8oz) onions, skinned and chopped
2 cloves garlic, peeled and chopped
$1\frac{1}{2}$ teaspoons ground cummin
1 tablespoon ground coriander
$\frac{1}{4}$ teaspoon baking powder
$\frac{1}{4}$ teaspoon cayenne pepper
Salt and freshly ground black pepper
$\frac{3}{4}$ bunch flat-leafed continental parsley, if available,
   trimmed, washed and drained, *or* use ordinary
   parsley
Vegetable oil for deep-frying

Rinse and drain the beans then place in a food processor or blender and process until almost smooth, but still grainy. Add all the remaining ingredients, except the parsley, and process again until finely chopped. Lastly, add the parsley and blend briefly so it is still identifiable. (The real thing, as I remember it, is quite grainy and not pasty, with the chopped greenery quite visible.) Let the mixture rest for 1 hour. Take a tablespoon of it at a time and make round flattened patties about 5cm (2in) in diameter. Deep fry them in the hot vegetable oil until crisp and golden all over. Drain and serve.

Peynerli Patlican
Aubergine Cheese Sandwiches

Although a little fiddly, these are well worth the effort.
Prepare and fry the aubergines in advance to make the task
easier.

> 675g (1½lb) aubergines (2 medium ones), trimmed
>   and washed
> 4 eggs
> 225g (8oz) ricotta cheese, *or* Greek Cypriot Aneri
>   cheese, *or* cream cheese, but not cottage cheese
> 30g (1oz) grated Parmesan cheese *or* Gruyère
>   cheese
> 3 tablespoons chopped mixed herbs, such as parsley,
>   mint, dill and chives
> 1 clove garlic, peeled and crushed
> Salt and freshly ground black pepper
> 150ml (5fl oz) groundnut oil *or* corn oil
> 110g (4oz) toasted breadcrumbs
> Sunflower oil for frying

Slice the aubergines in 0.6cm (¼in) thick rounds and immerse
in salted water as described on pages 112–13.

While they are soaking, prepare the filling. In a bowl, beat
two of the eggs lightly, add the cheeses, mash well and mix
with a fork. Add the chopped herbs and garlic, season
generously with salt and pepper and mix well.

Rinse and drain the aubergines, as described on page 113,
and dry them on a clean tea towel. In a frying pan, heat
the groundnut or corn oil and fry the aubergines on both
sides until light brown in colour. Remove and drain them
on absorbent kitchen towel. Discard the oil.

Halve each slice of aubergine, spread the filling thickly
on one half and sandwich neatly with the remaining half.
Press them lightly together.

Put the breadcrumbs in a large, shallow dish. In a clean frying pan, heat the sunflower oil. Beat the two remaining eggs in a wide bowl and dip each aubergine sandwich in it. Roll them immediately in the breadcrumbs, making sure they are well coated. Fry them in the oil, turning them over once, for 3 minutes altogether, until crisp and golden. Drain on absorbent kitchen towel. Serve them hot on a platter with a sprinkling of finely chopped herbs, such as fresh dill or parsley and mint.

Buñuelos de Alcachofas
Artichoke Fritters

SPAIN

Buñuelos can be sweet or savoury. They make excellent appetizers, and other kinds of vegetables such as carrots, kholrabi, or turnips can also be used.

    45g (1½oz) plain flour, sifted
    1 egg yolk
    4 tablespoons beer
    1 teaspoon olive oil
    Salt
    4 globe artichoke hearts (see page 105)
    2 tablespoons lemon juice
    Vegetable oil for deep-frying
    Lemon wedges to garnish

Place the first five ingredients in a bowl and beat well, then let the mixture stand for 30 minutes.

Cook the artichoke hearts in boiling water with the lemon juice for 3–5 minutes, according to their size, until tender, then drain. Quarter them and coat a few at a time in the batter. Remove with a slotted spoon and fry in hot vegetable oil until crisp and golden. Serve immediately with some lemon wedges.

Fiori Di Zucchini Ripieni
Stuffed Courgette Flowers

Stuffed courgette flowers are a prize in any cuisine, and although this recipe comes from Italy they are a delicacy that appears in Turkish and Greek cuisine also. They are well worth the trouble taken, from the excitement one derives from picking these beautiful creamy and orange-edged, miniature, lily-like flowers in the early morning, to the actual work of filling them, which is more like putting the final intricate stitches in a Venetian tapestry.

The flowers should ideally be picked early in the morning before the sun touches them as they will then close up. Trim the tiny green leaves at the base, wipe them a little and check for any insects. There is no need to wash them if they come from a familiar pesticide-free garden. In Italy and Greece one often sees courgettes for sale in the markets with their flowers still attached to them. If bought in a market it is best to wash the flowers quickly under running water and dry them.

57

FILLING

1 medium onion, skinned and grated finely
110g (4oz) long-grain rice, washed and drained
2 slices of peeled aubergine, soaked in salted water
   and diced finely
2 tablespoons finely chopped fresh dill *or* parsley
2 medium tomatoes, peeled, de-seeded and diced or
   grated
4 tablespoons olive oil
Salt
16 courgette flowers
120ml (4fl oz) olive oil

Mix all the filling ingredients in a bowl. Open each flower, gently extract the middle green stamen and discard, then fill each centre with the filling, and fold the petals over. In a wide saucepan that will accommodate all the flowers in one layer, place them on their sides, with the folded side against the sides of the saucepan. Once the outer circle has been filled, start an inner circle, trapping the folded sides against the flowers already in the pan.

Pour the 120ml (4fl oz) olive oil over the flowers, then add a very little water to barely reach halfway up their sides. Bring to the boil, cover and simmer for 15–20 minutes until the rice is tender but not overcooked.

Yalanci Dolma

Stuffed Vine Leaves

TURKEY

These 'pretend' dolmas are so-called because they do not contain any meat, therefore their appearance is deceptive. Nevertheless, they are enticing, and when quite aromatic they are, to my mind, better than the 'real' ones. These are served with bowls of plain (often home-made) thick, sheep's yoghurt.

225g (8oz) fresh or preserved vine leaves (about 45)
170g (6oz) long-grain rice, rinsed and drained
285g (10oz) grated onion
4 tablespoons chopped fresh mint or 1 tablespoon dried mint
3 tablespoons chopped fresh dill
55g (2oz) pine kernels, toasted first
Juice of ½ lemon
150ml (5fl oz), or a little more, olive oil
Salt and freshly ground black pepper
3 cloves garlic, peeled and halved
3 tablespoons tomato paste diluted in ½ a cup of hot water (optional)
300ml (10fl oz) hot water

Rinse and blanch 8–10 vine leaves at a time, for 1 minute. Remove from the water with a slotted spoon and drain. If using preserved leaves, rinse them and immerse in a bowl of hot water for 5 minutes. Remove them and rinse again as they are extremely salty, then drain.

In a large bowl, combine the rice, onion, herbs, pine kernels and lemon. Add half of the olive oil, season with salt and pepper and mix well.

Trim the stalks if needed, and flatten each vine leaf, with uneven side upwards. Place a tablespoon of stuffing near the serrated stem edge, fold that edge over it, then the left and right edges inwards and roll it into a small sausage-shape.

Line a large saucepan with 3–4 leaves, to prevent the dolmas sticking, and place them tightly in circles, and eventually layers, trapping the folded edges underneath. Stick garlic cloves in between, pour the rest of the oil over, the tomato paste if used (I personally prefer them without), and more seasoning. Place a small inverted plate on top to keep them in place while cooking and pour the water in at the edge. Bring to the boil, cover and cook gently for 50–55 minutes. Add 3–4 tablespoons water during cooking if necessary.

Biber Dolmasi
Stuffed Peppers

TURKEY/SYRIA

This is an exquisite stuffing, fragrant with spices and enriched with a mosaic of nuts. The use of olive oil is essential to the flavour of the dish. The saffron can be omitted rather than substituted with turmeric. If Basmati rice is used, the dish acquires an even more exotic taste.

Serves 6

6 large sweet peppers of mixed colours, washed and
    boiled briefly for 1—2 minutes
55g (2oz) pine kernels
85g (3oz) almonds
150ml (5fl oz) olive oil
2 large onions, skinned and sliced finely
170g (6oz) long-grain rice, preferably Basmati,
    rinsed, soaked and drained
¼ teaspoon allspice
½ teaspoon cinnamon
¼ teaspoon saffron strands, soaked in 2 tablespoons
    hot water
Salt and freshly ground black pepper
300ml (10fl oz) hot water
55g (2oz) *kus* uzumu — small currants
3 tablespoons finely chopped parsley
3 tablespoons olive oil

Slice the tops off the peppers and reserve. De-seed the peppers. Toast the pine kernels in a dry frying pan, turning constantly for 2 minutes until light golden in colour; take out and repeat this process with the almonds until they become quite aromatic.

In a large saucepan, heat the 150ml (5fl oz) olive oil, and fry the onion until golden in colour; add the drained rice, spices, salt and pepper and fry together, turning and coating the rice in the oil, for approximately 5 minutes.

Lower the heat, add half the hot water, mix well and as soon as the water is absorbed withdraw from heat and add nuts, currants and parsley.

Fill the peppers with this mixture, seal them with their reserved tops, and place in an ovenproof casserole so that they fit closely together. Mix the remaining water with the 3 tablespoons of olive oil and dribble over the peppers. Add some seasoning and cook uncovered in a preheated oven, gas no. 5 (375°F/190°C), for 50 minutes, basting occasionally.

Patlican Karni Yarik
Baked Aubergines with Meat Stuffing

TURKEY

The dish of aubergines that I enjoyed most during a recent trip to Turkey was at a restaurant in Kadikoy, Istanbul; the aubergines had been threaded with kebabs and cooked on charcoal, and their flesh was then piled over the meat inside an exquisitely thin flat bread.

Karni yarik, which literally means 'slit stomach', is similar to *Imam Bayildi* but with a meat stuffing.

61

4—5 thin, pale mauve aubergines *or* 2 large round
  ones
150ml (5fl oz) sunflower oil
1 green or red pepper, cored, de-seeded and cut in
  strips
1 medium onion, skinned and sliced finely
3 tablespoons olive oil
450g (1lb) minced lamb *or* beef
$\frac{1}{4}$ teaspoon allspice
$\frac{1}{4}$ teaspoon cinnamon
285g (10oz) tomatoes, peeled and chopped
3 tablespoons finely chopped parsley
150ml (5fl oz) water
Salt and freshly ground black pepper
1 tablespoon tomato purée diluted in a cup of hot
  water

Keep the aubergines whole, including their stems, and wash
them. Slit them lengthways on one side and only halfway
through, to make a pouch. If using the large round variety,
just slice them in half lengthways. Immerse them in a bowl
of salted water for 30 minutes; rinse and dry.

In a frying pan, heat the sunflower oil and fry the
aubergines slowly until pale golden in colour, then drain on
absorbent kitchen towel. If using the halved, round variety,
scoop a little of the flesh out from the middle of each piece,
to form a hollow. The extracted flesh should be chopped
and added to the meat later. Next, fry the pepper strips and
reserve.

In a saucepan, heat the olive oil and sauté the onion until
it becomes transparent. Mix in the meat and sauté together,
breaking up any lumps. Add all the remaining ingredients,
except the tomato purée, together with the aubergine flesh,
cover and cook for about 20 minutes, until quite dry.

Arrange the aubergines in an oven dish and fill the pouch-
like openings with the stuffing, or pile the stuffing on each
half aubergine; decorate with 1–2 strips of pepper. Pour the
diluted tomato purée into the base of the dish and cook in

a preheated oven, gas no. 4 (350°F/180°C), for 45 minutes, basting occasionally.

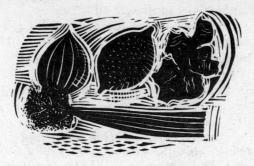

Patlican Tavasi
Baked Aubergines with Yoghurt

TURKEY

This delicious dish is served with the *mezze* but it also makes an excellent lunch.

> 675g (1½lb) aubergines, trimmed and sliced in
>   0.6cm (¼in) circles
> 150ml (5fl oz) vegetable oil for frying
> 140g (5oz) plain yoghurt
> 2 cloves garlic, peeled and crushed
> 2 tablespoons olive oil
> Salt

Soak and drain aubergines as described on pages 112–13, then dry them on a clean tea towel. In a frying pan, heat the vegetable oil and fry the aubergines until light golden in colour on both sides. Drain on absorbent paper. Arrange them in a medium-sized baking dish. Beat the yoghurt, garlic, olive oil and salt together and spread over the aubergines. Place in a preheated oven, gas no. 2 (300°F/150°C), for 15 minutes, to warm through.

PIES

Börek, Breiks, Bourekakia, Sanbusak
Small Savoury Pies

TURKEY/GREECE/YUGOSLAVIA/
MIDDLE EAST/NORTH AFRICA

Börek are intricate little parcels of pastry filled with all kinds of delicacies. They are an essential part of celebratory *mezze* and are suitable for any gathering.

All kinds of fillings can be used, meat with fragrant spices, pine nuts and currants, chicken and various vegetables; the most familiar ones, however, are the cheese or cheese and spinach fillings. In Greece, where wild *horta* – greens – gathering is a tradition, anything green from the autumnal hills goes into them.

The most common pastry used is the exquisitely thin pastry called *fyllo* – leaf – in Greek. In Turkey, the common *börek* pastry is *yufka* which are round sheets, softer, more pliable and slightly thicker than *fyllo*. And in North Africa it is the thin, irregular *ouarka* which is used for their delicious *breiks*. And of course there are the simple home-made pastries, often made from just plain flour and water, or sometimes containing olive oil and/or yoghurt.

Ready-made *fyllo* pastry is an excellent substitute if you don't want to make your own, and produces impressive results. It is available in 450g (1lb) packets and it can be kept in a freezer for up to four months. It needs two hours at room temperature to defrost. Using it is quite easy, if a little fiddly to begin with. Once it is unwrapped, be swift as *fyllo* dries quickly and becomes brittle. If you have not used it before, cover it with a clean, wet tea towel and take your time.

Fyllo can be used in whole sheets for the larger pies, such

as the Greek *kolokythopitta* (page 69) and the *baklava* (page ̄
or cut into strips to make the smaller pies. Different shapes
are explained in the individual recipes but here are the
instructions for the little triangular Turkish *börek*, universal
in the Middle East. For approximately fifteen *börek* use about
eight sheets of pastry and cut into four elongated strips of
8cm (3in) wide. Using two sheets at a time, brush the top
sheet with melted butter, place a teaspoon of filling in one
corner and fold over as shown in the diagram overleaf, to
make small triangles. Place on an oiled baking sheet, loose
ends trapped underneath, brush the tops with melted butter
and bake in a preheated oven, gas no. 4 (350°F/180°C), for
30 minutes, until crisp and light golden.

Spanakopittakia

Little Spinach Pies

These triangular little pies can be prepared in the same way
as *böreks* on page 66. Prepare the filling in advance and
assemble about one hour before they are to be served.

> 450g (1lb) fresh spinach, *or* 285g (10oz) packet
>   frozen leaf spinach
> 4 tablespoons olive oil
> 1 medium onion, skinned and sliced finely
> 110g (4oz) *feta* cheese, crumbled
> 2 medium eggs, beaten lightly
> 2 tablespoons finely chopped fresh dill *or* parsley
> Salt
> 8 sheets *fyllo* pastry
> 85g (3oz) melted butter for brushing over the
>   pastry

If using fresh spinach, wash it meticulously until no trace of grit remains, then drain it and chop coarsely. Place the raw spinach in a saucepan without any additional water, cover and cook over medium heat for 4–5 minutes, stirring occasionally. Drain and squeeze out its moisture. If using frozen spinach, defrost and drain it, then chop coarsely.

In a frying pan, heat the olive oil and lightly sauté the onion. Place in a bowl with all the remaining ingredients except the butter. Mix in the spinach. The mixture should be fairly thick.

Prepare the *fyllo* pastry as described on page 65. Place a heaped teaspoon of filling on each narrow sheet of *fyllo* pastry and fold as shown in the diagram beneath. Place on an oiled baking sheet, brush each pie with melted butter, and bake in a preheated oven, gas no. 4 (350°F/180°C), for 30 minutes, until crisp and golden.

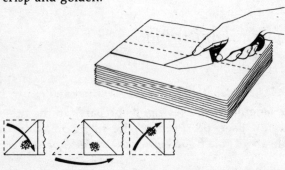

VARIATION

Tyropittakia
Little Cheese Pies

GREECE

Use the same filling ingredients as in the recipe for *tyropittakia Lefteritsas* on page 68 and prepare in little triangular *börek* as above.

Patates Börek

Little Potato Pastries

This recipe was given to me by my cousin Ivi in Istanbul.
It is quite a grand and extremely appetizing dish, particularly
because of the method by which she encloses the filling,
using the soft, ready-made, Turkish *yufka* pastry. She uses
three sheets of pastry, dividing the filling (but double the
quantities given below) between the first and second sheets,
spreading it evenly over them. She covers this with the third
sheet and rolls it firmly like a thick sausage. It is then wrapped
in a clean tea towel and put in the refrigerator where, as
it cools down, it acquires its firm shape. It is then sliced
thinly into 1cm (½in) discs and fried in hot oil, until crisp
and golden on both sides. Here I have substituted with *fyllo*
pastry, resulting in larger pies.

FILLING

450g (1lb) potatoes, peeled, washed and cut in large
   cubes
55g (2oz) butter
Salt and freshly ground black pepper
110g (4oz) *feta* cheese, crumbled
2 eggs
2—3 tablespoons chopped parsley

PASTRY

225g (8oz) *fyllo* pastry
55g (2oz) melted butter
150ml (5fl oz) or more sunflower oil for frying

Boil the potatoes until soft, drain and mash. Mix with butter,
seasoning and cheese, while hot, so the butter melts and
is well incorporated. Add the eggs one by one, mixing well

after each addition, and lastly add the parsley. Let the filling cool before using it.

Make triangle pastries as described on page 65. In a large frying pan, heat the vegetable oil (hot but not smoking) and fry them for 2 minutes on each side, until crisp and light golden. Drain on absorbent paper and serve immediately.

Tyropittakia Lefteritsas
Little Cheese Pies

These delicious cheese pies are made by the mother of a friend of mine in Athens, whose name is Eleftheria, and we have always called them after her.

Their difference is the rich, crumbly pastry which, unlike other pastries, is easy to make and roll out (olive oil is the trick), even if pastry is not your strong point. Makes about 15.

PASTRY

200g (7oz) self-raising flour, sifted
4 tablespoons olive oil
2 tablespoons melted butter *or* margarine
85g (3oz) plain thick yoghurt

FILLING

140g (5oz) *feta* cheese, crumbled with a fork
1 large egg, lightly beaten
2 tablespoons finely chopped fresh dill *or* mint *or* 1
    tablespoon dried mint
1 tablespoon finely chopped chives, *or* the green
    part of a spring onion
Freshly ground black pepper

TOPPING

1 egg yolk, lightly beaten

To make the pastry, just mix all the pastry ingredients together in a large bowl until well incorporated. Add a little more flour if the mixture is too wet. Cover and let it rest for 15 minutes in the refrigerator.

In the meantime, combine all the filling ingredients in a bowl to produce a thick mixture.

Take walnut-sized pieces of pastry and roll them out on a lightly-floured surface. Cut circles of about 8cm (3in) diameter, using a glass or a teacup. Place a teaspoon of filling along the middle of each circle of dough, fold over to make a little half-moon shape, and press the edges together to seal them. Place on a buttered baking sheet. Using a brush or a piece of kitchen paper, brush the pies with the beaten egg yolk, and cook in a preheated oven, gas no. 5 (375°F/ 190°C), for 20 minutes, until light golden and crisp on top. Serve hot. They also remain delicious when cold the next day, which makes them ideal for a picnic.

Kolokythopitta
A Courgette Pie

GREECE

This is quite an unusual pie with a delicious filling. The recipe was given to me by a friend who comes from the Ionian island of Corfu. It can be served either as a first course or as a main meal accompanied by a substantial crisp green salad.

Serves 4—6

FILLING

560g (1¼lb) courgettes, trimmed, washed and
  scraped lightly
55g (2oz) long-grain rice, rinsed and drained
1 medium onion, skinned and grated thickly
3—4 spring onions, sliced finely
85g (3oz) freshly grated Parmesan cheese, Gruyère
  or Cheddar cheese
3 eggs, lightly beaten
4 tablespoons olive oil
2 tablespoons each of chopped fresh dill and parsley
Salt and freshly ground black pepper

PASTRY

450g (1lb) (1 packet) *fyllo* pastry
110g (4oz) butter, melted

Grate the courgettes thickly. Place them in a bowl and mix
with all the remaining filling ingredients.

Using a pastry brush, butter the top sheet of pastry and
line the base of an oiled, medium-sized, roasting dish, folding
any excess lengthways edges at alternate ends; or, measure
the roasting dish against the pastry and trim its length only,
allowing also 10cm (4in) for shrinkage. Continue in the same
fashion, laying each sheet as neatly as you can, until about
half the pastry has been used.

Spread the filling evenly on top of the pastry and fold
all four pastry sides over, to contain the filling. Cover with
the remaining pastry, buttering each sheet first, and then
butter the top sheet liberally. Trim excess edges or tuck them
in at the sides.

Using a sharp knife, cut the top layers of pastry only
(otherwise the filling might spill) into square or diamond
shapes, approximately 8 x 5cm (3 x 2in). Using the tips of

your fingers, sprinkle a little cold water on top of the pastry, to prevent the *fyllo* curling up at the edges.

Bake in a preheated oven, gas no. 5 (375°F/190°C), for 45 minutes until crisp and light golden.

Ricotta and Olive Pie

A delicious pie, which resembles a French quiche but with an unusual filling. The same method can be used with different fillings, for instance the Moroccan *zaalouk* mixed with 2 beaten eggs (page 51), or spinach and cheese as in the Greek pies, or the potato and cheese filling of the Turkish *patates börek* (page 67).

PASTRY

200g (7oz) plain flour, sifted
Pinch of salt
110g (4oz) cold butter, cubed
3—4 tablespoons cold water

FILLING

225g (8oz) ricotta, cream cheese *or* Greek
  Cypriot *aneri* cheese
85g (3oz) freshly grated Parmesan cheese
85g (3oz) toasted breadcrumbs
2 eggs, lightly beaten
3 tablespoons single cream *or* milk
110g (4oz) green olives, stoned and halved
30g (1oz) pine kernels, toasted first
15g (½ oz) butter, melted
Salt and freshly ground black pepper

71

Combine the flour and salt in a bowl and, using your fingertips, rub in the cold butter for a few minutes, until the mixture resembles breadcrumbs. Add enough cold water to form a firm dough, knead it a little, make into a ball and cover, then rest the dough in the refrigerator for 15 minutes.

Butter a 26cm (10in) quiche dish. Roll the pastry out onto a lightly-floured surface, into a circle a little larger than the base of the dish. Roll the pastry onto the rolling pin, and line the base and sides of the dish. Trim excess edges. Prick the pastry with a fork and bake in a preheated oven, gas no. 6 (400°F/200°C), for 10 minutes.

In the meantime, place the ricotta cheese (or whichever cheese you are using) in a bowl and mash it with a fork until all lumps have gone and it is smooth and creamy. Add the remaining ingredients and mix well.

Spread the mixture evenly in the half-baked pastry case. Turn the oven down to gas no. 5 (375°F/190°C) and bake for a further 30–35 minutes.

Briks à L'oeuf

Egg Pastries

TUNISIA

These are the archetypal crisp savoury pastries, with the combination of the unexpected filling and its soft pleasing consistency, literally exploding in the mouth.

They can be made in different shapes but for expedience I prefer to make cylindrical, elongated parcels enclosing a soft vegetable, chicken, meat or fish filling, with a raw egg neatly broken into a well in the centre. Any kind of soft, but not too juicy, filling from the vegetable section can also be used as a base for the raw egg to nest in. For instance, the Moroccan *zaalouk* with aubergines (page 51) is an ideal alternative, or a French *ratatouille* (page 121).

In this particular recipe there is a combination of fish and raw egg. The fish can be canned tuna or any fresh fish steak such as halibut, cod, haddock or turbot, lightly poached first, skinned, boned and flaked.

These little pastries should ideally be eaten using one's fingers and not a knife and fork, to safeguard against the possibility of the mellow egg filling dribbling everywhere!

They are unexpectedly unusual which makes them always quite a success.

Serves 6

FILLING

4 tablespoons corn oil *or* sunflower oil
2 medium onions, skinned and diced finely
2 cloves garlic, peeled and crushed
198g (7oz) can of tuna, drained and shredded
3 tablespoons finely chopped parsley
Juice of ½ lemon
Salt and freshly ground black pepper
6 eggs

PASTRY

8 sheets of *fyllo* pastry
150ml (5fl oz) or more vegetable oil for frying
1 lemon, quartered

To make the filling, heat the corn or sunflower oil in a frying pan and soften the onions until golden, then add the garlic and stir very briefly until just aromatic. Mix with all the remaining filling ingredients, except the eggs, and set aside.

Fold a sheet of pastry in the middle lengthways, place 1–1½ tablespoons of filling along one end, make a well in the filling and neatly break a raw egg into it, without mixing it up. Season and quickly fold the edge of pastry over; fold the two sides over it inwards, to seal and protect the filling, and roll up gently until the remaining length of pastry has been folded round it. Continue in the same fashion with the remaining pastry and filling.

In a large frying pan, heat 2.5cm (1in) of vegetable oil (it should be hot but not smoking) and slide 2–3 of the pastries gently in it. Cook for about 2 minutes on each side, until crisp and light golden. Take out with a slotted spoon and serve immediately with lemon quarters.

Pissaladière
Onion, Tomato and Anchovy Tart

FRANCE/PROVENCE

Pissaladière, the nearest equivalent to an Italian *pizza*, can also be made without the tomatoes but, to my taste at least, it then lacks the moist and sugary balance it needs.

Serves 6

200ml (7fl oz) warm water
½ teaspoon sugar
8g (¼oz) fresh yeast *or* halve the quantity for dried yeast
25g (8oz) plain flour, sifted
¾ teaspoon salt
1 tablespoon olive oil

TOPPING

120ml (4fl oz) olive oil
1kg (2lb) onions, skinned and sliced finely
Salt and freshly ground black pepper
2 cloves garlic, peeled and crushed
450g (1lb) ripe tomatoes, peeled, de-seeded and
chopped
1 teaspoon dried thyme and a few leaves of fresh
basil, if available, chopped finely
8 canned anchovy fillets, drained or, if salted,
rinsed and soaked in water for 10 minutes
110g (4oz) black olives, stoned (ideally the wrinkled
oily variety)

Put the warm water in a bowl, add the sugar and yeast and dissolve. Let it rest in a warm place until frothy. Place the flour in a bowl, make a well in the centre and add the yeast, salt and olive oil. Start mixing it from the centre, drawing in and incorporating the flour, working outwards. Once it has formed a soft dough, place it onto a floured, flat surface and knead vigorously, pulling and folding it, for 5 minutes, until smooth and quite elastic. Cover it with a clean, damp tea towel and leave in a warm place for about 1 hour until it has almost doubled in volume.

In a frying pan, heat the olive oil and sauté the onion gently until pale golden in colour; add seasoning, cover and cook for 20 minutes until very soft, stirring occasionally. Add the garlic for the last 1–2 minutes.

Punch and knead the dough briefly, once it has risen, to knock out the air. With your fingers, press the dough to line the base of an oiled 30cm (12in) baking sheet. Spread the onion mixture evenly on top, sprinkle the tomatoes and herbs over and season with some pepper. Decorate with the drained anchovies, making a lattice design, and place an olive in each section. Bake in a preheated oven, gas no. 5 (375°F/190°C), for 30 minutes until nicely browned on top. Slice into rectangular or square pieces and serve hot or at room temperature.

PICKLES AND SAUCES

Badhinjan Mukhallal

Aubergine Pickle

Take medium-sized egg-plants, cut off half the stalks
and leaf: then half boil in salt and water, take out
and dry. Cut firmly, and stuff with fresh celery
leaves, a few sprigs of mint, and some quarters of
peeled garlic. Put in layers in a glass bottle, sprinkle
with aromatic herbs and fine-brayed *blattes de Byzance*,
and cover with good vinegar. Leave until quite
matured: then use. (Professor A. J. Arberry, 'A
Baghdad cookery book'.)

Badingan Turshussu
Aubergine Pickle

TURKEY

This is a recipe from *A Turkish Cookery Book* by Turabi Effendi,
published in 1862. It is identical to the medieval *Badhinjan
Mukhallal* above and, more important, the method is identical
to the ways used for pickling tiny aubergines nowadays
throughout the Eastern Mediterranean and the Balkans.

Procure as many egg-plants as are required, take the
stalks off, split each one in three or four lengthways,
without separating from the bottom, and scald them;
then place them in a wicker-basket one over the
other, put a piece of board or a plate over them,
over which place an iron weight, and let them remain
for eight or ten hours, so as to draw the bitter water

from them. Then chop up some parsley and celery, which mix with one or two dozen cloves of garlic, each cut in two; then stuff between each slice of the egg-plants with the ingredients and tie up each of the egg-plants with the stalks of celery, to prevent the stuffing from falling out; then arrange them in a stone jar one over the other, cover them with wine vinegar, place a piece of clean board over, and on the top an iron weight to press it; let it remain for about three weeks: it is then ready for use.

It would suffice, I think, to say that this was made by my grandmother, a refugee from Smyrna, until her last days, about eight years ago, in an identical manner and that it is the best pickle ever made.

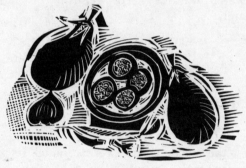

Pesto
Basil Sauce

Pesto combines the most characteristic of Mediterranean ingredients. In the land where round heads of tender basil grow with the sweetest of scents, it would have been difficult to pass by without enhancing the bubbling kitchen pots with its presence. *Pesto* can be served with all kinds of pasta, but it is also delicious with vegetables such as boiled new potatoes, carrots or courgettes. It is enchanting when served *al fresco*, preferably under a vine.

1½ teacups basil leaves
2 cloves garlic, peeled and chopped
2 tablespoons pine kernels
1½ tablespoons freshly grated Parmesan cheese
1 tablespoon freshly grated Sardinian *pecorino*
  cheese
5 tablespoons good quality olive oil
Salt
3 tablespoons hot (but not boiling) water

In a food processor or blender, combine all the ingredients
except the water, and blend until creamy. Mix with the hot
water just before the sauce is to be served.

Cook 225g (8oz) of pasta, uncovered, in a pan of salted
boiling water until *al dente*. Toss gently in the sauce and serve
immediately.

Béchamel Sauce

Béchamel is the sauce that transforms and uplifts plain dishes.
A thin layer of it over any collection of sautéed vegetables,
with some cheese or breadcrumbs sprinkled on top to give
pungency and texture once baked, can turn the simplest of
ingredients into a desirable meal or first course.

45g (1½oz) butter
55g (2oz) plain flour
600ml (1 pint) hot milk
Salt and white pepper
1 egg yolk, lightly beaten

In a medium saucepan, melt the butter over a low heat
without browning it. Add the flour and cook slowly, stirring

constantly for 1–2 minutes. Remove from the heat, add the hot, but not boiling, milk and beat with a wire whisk, scraping the sides with a spatula, until it has all been properly blended. Add the seasoning, return to a medium heat and cook for a further 4–5 minutes, beating constantly until thickened to the desired consistency. (If a thick sauce is required, cook it a little longer.) Remove from the heat, add the egg slowly, beating at the same time, and return to a gentle heat for a further minute.

Neapolitan Pomarola Sauce
A deliciously Italian Tomato Sauce

ITALY

Perhaps the most characteristic of Italian sauces, and most commonly used, is this Neapolitan favourite. Used primarily with pasta but also with pizza and all kinds of baked vegetables, it is unmistakeably summery, unmistakeably Mediterranean, a real favourite with everyone and more so with children. When made with fresh, ripe tomatoes, it is in a class by itself, but it is excellent with canned tomatoes too, and it also freezes well. Whenever a recipe calls for half a portion of *pomarola* sauce, it is still advantageous to cook the full portion and freeze the rest.

> 2 × 396g (14oz) cans of tomatoes, *or* 1kg (2lb) ripe
>   tomatoes, peeled and de-seeded
> 60ml (2fl oz) olive oil
> 2 cloves garlic, peeled and sliced finely
> 1/4 teaspoon sugar
> 1 teaspoon dried oregano
> Salt and freshly ground black pepper
> Some fresh basil leaves if available

In a food processor or blender, liquidize the contents of the cans of tomatoes. If using fresh tomatoes, chop finely, or grate them.

In a saucepan, heat the olive oil and sauté the garlic without browning it, then add all the remaining ingredients, except the fresh basil. Cover and cook for 30 minutes, stirring occasionally. Chop and add the fresh basil after this time; the sauce should be smooth and thick by then, as most of the water will have evaporated. You can then use it as required in each recipe.

SOUPS

Minestrone di Carciofi alla Siciliana

Sicilian Minestrone of Globe Artichokes

Minestrone, basically a thick, seasonal vegetable soup, changes as one travels up and down the Italian autostradas, with the precision and frequency of an eloquent and vain female. In the north it is fragrant with fresh herbs and often has the addition of rice instead of the more familiar pasta. Further south, in central Italy and safely at home (as Genoa bears serious claims over its creation), it becomes assertively robust with the addition of beans and, in an exquisite regional variation, is engulfed in the folds of aromatic Genoese *pesto* just before it is served, which makes it a memorable affair, challenged only by the almost identical Provençal dish of *soupe aux pistou* (page 94). In the Mediterranean south, garlic and tomatoes unavoidably predominate, and in Sicily we came across an unexpected and voluptuous form of this soup: a *minestrone* consisting mainly of soft, mouth-melting, fresh globe artichokes, the noble relative of the imperially-coloured thistles.

In May 1973, on the island of Salina, off the Sicilian coast, we settled for lunch on a magnificent terrace, high above the flickering waters sparkling in the sunshine. Around us was a sharply rolling ragged landscape, dry already from the burning sun and rich only in astoundingly large, pale pink flowers of the abundant caper plants. Immediately underneath us, the small terraced gardens of our Italian friend's house were bordered with a few olive trees, two or three almond trees and a huge mulberry, which gave shelter to the invisible cicadas. Across the table I faced the most awe-inspiring background to a lunch I have ever seen; the sharp, granitic peak of Mount Etna, precariously luxurious, floating out of the shimmering waters, innocently garlanded by soft whirls of volcanic smoke. Immediately behind me, from the brilliantly white-washed kitchen, whiffs of the most delicate and subtle aroma intermingled with the smell of sharp wood burning on the fire on which the burly housekeeper, Giordano, and his wife had been cooking, in the typical primitive corner hearth. The surprise of the day, an artichoke soup which, judging by the ingredients that jostled themselves in the stillness of the morning on the verandah table and in and out of blackened pots in the kitchen, could only be delectable. As the morning grew on, the stillness had been broken by the regular snapping of the artichoke leaves, the mountains of green debris growing all around us. With an investigative eye I had followed the entire happenings of the morning. I had seen the tender chicken breasts abruptly separated from the bone in two decisive movements, and then gently sliced into paper-thin fillets. I had spied on Giordano's wife disappearing among the garden undergrowth, collecting here and there her valuable ingredients: a few young, brightly coloured carrots, some green celery leaves, woody sprigs of unidentifiable wild herbs, etc. Finally, there could be no mistaking from the vigour with which she attacked the huge, silvery, furry bush of the sage plant that this would play a protagonist's part in the midday performance.

But the search had not yet been concluded; and as we were all admiring her trophies on the huge verandah table, we were startled by what sounded like a shot that rent the morning air as Mrs Giordano – arms thrown in the air – with a mystifying warrior's cry 'Prezzemolo, Prezzemolo', threw herself from the edge of the verandah, into the abyss as far as I was concerned, headscarf flowing one way and her black hair unwinding in the opposite direction, looking for a brief moment in her grave desperation like the winged

84

Victory of Samothraki (perhaps a little shorter and certainly much stouter) caught in midair. As my Italian vocabulary, brief at the time, did not include this danger cry of *'Prezzemolo, Prezzemolo'*, it caught me totally unawares and I presumed to my horror that either the family of snakes, nesting in the garden well, that terrorized Mrs Giordano, had at last made their dramatic exit, or that the undergrowth was on fire. A moment later, we found that she had landed unscathed on the semi-scorched patch of parsley that lay underneath, and in an instant stroke of brilliance I decoded her 'warrior's' cry: she had forgotten the parsley, a grievous error to any serious Italian cook.

Since our second course was going to be a light one of the chicken breast fillets, sautéed in butter with sage and garlic, the rest of the chicken carcass was already bubbling with carrots, onion, celery and some herbs in order to prepare a light broth for the soup which was obviously the glittering event of the meal.

We later had the same soup in one of the restaurants crowning the harbour in Palermo, but by then it had acquired the southern vigour and it had become a more familiar and sturdy affair, with garlic and tomatoes, lacking the finesse with which it had been handled in Salina by our hosts. The chicken broth was missing and flavour had been supplemented by sautéed cubes of *pancetta*, the salted, cured, unsmoked pork that resembles salami.

Allow at least one globe artichoke per person, more if you can endure the labour of their preparation. If you lack chicken broth, which could be made from chicken wings, necks or bones, substitute with four or five slices of unsmoked bacon, shredded. Any kind of small pasta can be used, allowing roughly a tablespoon per person.

5 artichokes
lemon juice
1.4 litres (2½ pints) chicken broth *or* hot water *and*
    4—5 slices unsmoked bacon, shredded
5 tablespoons olive oil
1 large onion, skinned and sliced thinly
1 small strip of celery with some leaves, trimmed
    and shredded
85g (3oz) small pasta
3 tablespoons of roughly chopped parsley
Salt and freshly ground black pepper
55g (2oz) freshly grated Parmesan cheese

Prepare the artichokes as described on page 105 and slice them thickly. Place them in water with a little lemon juice to prevent discolouring.

If you are not using chicken broth, sauté the shredded bacon in the olive oil in a large saucepan. Add the onions, celery and artichokes and sauté without browning, turning them for 2–3 minutes until they glisten. Add broth or hot water, cover and simmer for about 15 minutes. Add the pasta, parsley and seasoning and cook for a further 6–8 minutes. Sprinkle over the Parmesan just before serving and mix well.

Sopa De Ajo
Castilian Garlic Soup

It, however, agrees well with the peasants, as does the soup of their neighbours the Catalans, which is made of bread and garlic in equal portions fried in oil and diluted with hot water. This mess is called *Sopa de gato*, probably from making cats, not Catalans, sick. (Richard Ford)

In this rather unkind spirit, Richard Ford treated harshly the Spanish Garlic Soup, a national dish in distant days of sobriety and culinary introversion. However, most Spaniards are still fond of this dish and treat it differently, so read on! Similar peasant soups are common in France such as the *soupe à l'ail* of Languedoc or the *aigo boulido* of Provence.

My friend Ange de Vena has described with fond memories the way this soup used to be served regularly for breakfast at her grandparents' house in Granja de Moreruela near Zamora. This is their way of making it:

        4 cloves garlic, peeled and crushed
        1 teaspoon paprika
        ¼ teaspoon cayenne pepper
        120ml (4fl oz) olive oil
        900ml (1½ pints) water
        Salt
        4 thin slices of stale bread
        4 eggs
        1 teaspoon finely chopped parsley

Combine the first four ingredients in a bowl and mix well. Bring the water and salt to the boil in a saucepan, add the garlic mixture and stir well. Cover and simmer for 15 minutes then add the bread and cook for a further five minutes. Take the slices out and place one in each plate.

Carefully break the eggs one by one and slide them into the saucepan, over gentle heat. Poach them for 2–3 minutes then, using a slotted spoon, remove and serve one on each slice of bread. Ladle the soup on top and sprinkle over a little parsley.

An alternative way is to sauté the crushed garlic lightly in the olive oil first with a crushed dry red chilli; then continue as above.

Gazpacho

Any remarks on Spanish salad would be incomplete without some account of *gazpacho*, that vegetable soup, or floating salad, which during the summer forms the food of the bulk of the people in the torrid portions of Spain. This dish is of Arabic origin, as its name, 'soaked bread', implies. This most ancient Oriental, Roman and Moorish refection is composed of onions, garlic, cucumbers, chilis, all chopped up very small and mixed with crumbs of bread, and then put into a bowl of oil, vinegar, and fresh water. Reapers and agricultural labourers could never stand the sun's fire without this cooling acetous diet. This was the *oxikratos* of the Greeks, the *posca*, potable food, meat and drink, *potus et esca*, which formed part of the rations of the Roman soldiers, and which Adrian (a Spaniard) delighted to share with them, and into which Boaz at mealtime invited Ruth to dip her morsel. Dr Buchanan found some Syrian Christians who still called it *ail, ail, Hil, Hila*, for which our saviour was supposed to have called on the Cross, when those who understood that dialect gave it him from the vessel which was full of it for the guard.

In Andalusia, during the summer, a bowl of *gazpacho* is commonly ready in every house of an evening, and is partaken of by every person who comes in. It is not easily digested by strangers, who do not require so much as the natives, whose souls are more parched and dried up, and who perspire less. (Richard Ford)

Gazpachos are versatile, with numerous variations, and, although their aim is to refresh after the scalding Andalusian heat, come the first days of rain in September and the impending coolness in the air, the typical *gazpacho* made with tomatoes is also served hot. This is simply achieved by adding hot water to the same ingredients and increasing the volume of bread to make the soup more substantial. There is also a winter version which is particularly popular with peasants working in the fields; this is called *gazpacho caliente* and contains olive oil, garlic, soaked bread and orange juice.

Serves 4—6

675g (1½lb) sweet, ripe tomatoes, peeled, de-seeded and chopped
Piece of cucumber, 9cm (3in) long, peeled and chopped
2 cloves garlic, peeled and crushed
1 large sweet pepper, either green or red, cored, de-seeded and coarsely chopped
110g (4oz) crustless bread soaked in water and squeezed first
Salt and freshly ground black pepper
425ml (15fl oz) cold water
5 tablespoons olive oil
2 tablespoons white wine vinegar

GARNISHES

Cucumber, peeled and finely diced
Sweet pepper, peeled and finely diced
Tiny croutons, fried in olive oil

Mix the tomatoes, cucumber, garlic, sweet pepper, bread and seasoning with half the water in a food processor or liquidizer and liquidize in batches. With the machine still running, slowly add the olive oil and vinegar. Taste and adjust the seasoning, and empty the creamy soup into a large bowl. Slowly add the remaining water, stirring until it has all been incorporated. Cover and chill for 1–2 hours.

Place the garnishes in separate bowls and serve with the soup.

Gazpacho Blanco o Ajo Blanco

An Almond Gazpacho

SPAIN/CORDOBA, MALAGA, CADIZ

This smooth, milky-white *gazpacho* with fruit floating in it is quite untypical and unlike our familiar tomato one which is more robust. It is really a distant relative of the Greek garlic sauce *skorthalia*, diluted with water.

> 140g (5oz) white crustless bread
> 140g (5oz) whole almonds, blanched and peeled
> 2 cloves garlic, peeled and chopped
> 90ml (3fl oz) olive oil
> 3 tablespoons white wine vinegar
> Salt
> 425ml (15fl oz) cold water
> A few white grapes such as Muscatel, halved and seeded *or* cubes of melon or apple (optional)

Put the bread in a bowl, add some water and soak for 15 minutes. Grind the almonds and garlic in a food processor or blender, quite finely; with the machine still running, slowly add the olive oil and, when it thickens, the vinegar, the bread squeezed out lightly and some salt. Process together to a smooth white paste. Empty this into a bowl, mix with the cold water and chill.

Just before serving the *gazpacho*, float a few ice cubes and the fruit in it.

Zuppa Di Cecci

Chickpea Soup

One of the *Mevlevi* parables in Turkey draws on the chickpea.
  While being boiled, the chickpea jumps up, trying to get out of the saucepan, and screams and protests: 'Why do you do this to me?' The woman pushing it down with her wooden spoon says: 'I do this to you not because I hate you but because I want to make you delicious so that you may be eaten and then transformed into power of thought that discovers great truths. You had water in the garden to make you grow green and fresh and prepare you all along for the fire. You have left the soil to become food for the soul, power and thought ...'
  Nohut çorbasi in Turkey, *soupe aux pois chiches* in Languedoc, France, or *revithia soupa* in Greece, are all very similar substantial winter soups, with or without tomatoes. In France and Italy they prefer to liquidize either the whole or part of the soup, so that a creamy background supports it.

> 225g (8oz) chickpeas, picked clean and soaked
>   overnight
> 150ml (5fl oz) olive oil
> 1 clove garlic, peeled but left whole
> 396g (14oz) can tomatoes, drained and chopped
> 1 small sprig fresh rosemary
> Salt and freshly ground black pepper

Rinse and drain the chickpeas. Place in a medium-sized saucepan, cover them by about 2.5cm (1in) cold water, bring to the boil and skim until clear. Add all the remaining ingredients, cover and simmer for about 1 hour, or 20 minutes in a pressure cooker, until very tender.

Harira
Ramadan Soup

Harira is the soup that ends the daily fast during Ramadan in North Africa. The firing of a cannon at sunset is the signal for the long-awaited meal to start, along with all kinds of street festivities. Traditionally, as the groups of men gather in squares or teashops, wandering bards of the Homeric tradition perform, reciting legendary poems and songs in wailing voices, accompanied by a special single-string fiddle, the *rebab*.

Harira varies from family to family and region to region but it is always fragrant and colourful. Instead of rice, a wheat-shaped pasta (the Greek *kritharaki*, an ingredient in the Greek dish *yiouvetsi*) is often used, which traditionally was made at home from flour and water.

Serves 6

5 tablespoons good quality vegetable oil
2 medium onions, skinned and chopped
1 tablespoon peeled and grated fresh root ginger
½ teaspoon turmeric
¼ teaspoon ground cinnamon
450g (1lb) tomatoes, peeled and chopped
1.2 litres (2 pints) chicken stock *or* water
110g (4oz) chickpeas, soaked overnight, washed and drained
2 short sticks celery and leaves, trimmed, washed and chopped finely
1 large white radish, peeled and cubed
3 tablespoons finely chopped parsley
2 tablespoons finely chopped fresh coriander
Salt and freshly ground black pepper
55g (2oz) rice, washed and drained
Juice of ½ lemon

In a large saucepan or pressure cooker, heat the vegetable oil and sauté the onions until glistening. Add the ginger, turmeric and cinnamon and sauté together briefly. Mix in the tomatoes and, 2 minutes later, the stock or water; bring to a boil and add all the remaining ingredients except the rice and lemon juice. Cover and simmer for 1 hour (or 20 minutes in a pressure cooker), until the chickpeas are tender. Add the rice and cook for a further 10 minutes, then pour in the lemon juice and serve.

Fasolatha

Cannellini Bean Soup

GREECE

This is indisputably *the* national Greek dish, despite the feeble arguments from some middle-class metropolitan quarters. It is a thick, nourishing winter soup that features at family meals on Wednesdays or Fridays, typically the fasting days.

It is one of the best soups around the Mediterranean, wholly vegetarian and cheap (the main concern at all ages) but, above all, exceptionally delicious.

225g (8oz) *cannellini* beans, picked clean and soaked overnight
1 medium onion, skinned and sliced finely
2 medium carrots, trimmed, scraped and sliced in thin discs
1 celery stick with some leaves, trimmed, washed and sliced finely
396g (14oz) can tomatoes, chopped
1 tablespoon tomato purée
1 tablespoon dried oregano
150ml (5fl oz) olive oil
Salt and freshly ground black pepper
2 tablespoons chopped parsley

Rinse and drain the beans. Place them in a large saucepan, cover with cold water, bring to the boil and boil for 3 minutes. Drain, discarding the water. Cover them with about 4cm (1½in) of fresh water, add all the remaining ingredients, except the salt and parsley, and mix. Bring to the boil, add the salt, cover and simmer for about 1 hour until the beans are tender but not falling apart. If using a pressure cooker it will only take about 15 minutes. Cooking time can vary according to the quality and age of the beans. When beans are cooked, add the parsley, mix and cook for a further 1–2 minutes.

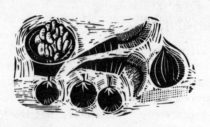

Soupe Au Pistou
Vegetable and Pasta Soup

FRANCE/PROVENCE

A wonderful summer soup, which I often make on the island of Alonnisos in the summer when I run out of ideas, since all the ingredients seem to be at hand. It is basically a relative of the Italian *minestrone* but with the addition of the basil-based Genoese *pesto* which the Niçois named in their local dialect, after the pestle used to make it, *pistou*.

La soupe au pistou contains a selection of summer vegetables, among which the most necessary are the *haricots frais*, which are not available in Britain unless home-grown but which can be substituted with dried haricot beans, soaked overnight and parboiled first. The *pistou* should be mixed into the soup off the heat, just before it is served.

Serves 6

SOUP

85g (3oz) haricot beans, cleaned and soaked
  overnight
4 tablespoons olive oil
1 onion, skinned and chopped finely
2 small leeks, prepared, washed and sliced thinly
450g (1lb) fresh tomatoes, peeled, de-seeded and
  chopped
1.2 litres (2 pints) water
225g (8oz) potatoes, peeled and cubed
170g (6oz) French green beans, trimmed and sliced
  in 2.5cm (1in) pieces
1 tablespoon mixed fresh thyme and marjoram,
  chopped *or* ½ teaspoon each dried thyme and
  marjoram
Salt and freshly ground black pepper
225g (8oz) courgettes, trimmed, washed and sliced
55g (2oz) spaghetti broken into 2.5cm (1in) lengths
2 tablespoons parsley, chopped finely

PISTOU

2 cloves garlic, peeled and chopped
¾ teacup of basil tops (leaves and tender stems)
55g (2oz) freshly grated Parmesan cheese
60ml (2fl oz) olive oil

First, make the soup. Put the haricot beans in a large saucepan, cover with cold water, bring to the boil, cover and simmer for 30 minutes. Drain, discarding their liquid.

In a large saucepan, heat the olive oil and sauté the onion and leeks until they glisten. Add the tomatoes and sauté for a further 1–2 minutes. Stir in the water and bring to the boil, then add all the remaining ingredients, except the courgettes, pasta and parsley. Cover and simmer for 20 minutes. Add the courgettes, and 5 minutes later mix in the pasta and parsley and cook for a further 10 minutes.

Place the garlic, basil and cheese in a food processor or blender and blend until smooth. Pour in the olive oil slowly and gradually until it has all been incorporated into a thick paste. Don't worry if the mixture separates, the flavour will still be alive and kicking. Stir the *pistou* into the soup and serve with fresh bread. It is a meal in itself.

Bamya Corbasi
Okra Soup

In Turkey, strings of tiny dried okra can be seen hanging like necklaces in all the markets. The okra is gathered when the plants need thinning at the beginning of the season. Dried okra is used in the winter in these traditional soups, which are often offered at the end of a meal. It is also used in meat casseroles like fresh okra. Although dried okra is not available, as far as I know, in Britain, one can substitute with fresh okra.

> 170g (6oz) dried okra, *or* 285g (10oz) fresh okra
> 2 small courgettes, trimmed, washed and scraped
> lightly
> 30g (1oz) butter
> 900ml (1½ pints) meat stock *or* chicken stock
> 2 tablespoons tomato purée
> Salt

If using dried okra, soak it in cold water overnight. Drain and discard the liquid. Wash and trim the fresh okra. Grate the courgettes thickly.

In a large saucepan, melt the butter and sauté the grated courgettes for 2–3 minutes. Add the stock, tomato purée and salt. Bring to the boil, then place the drained okra in the saucepan, cover and simmer for about 30 minutes, until tender.

Risi e Bisi
Rice and Peas

Venetians, among Italians, are the most passionate about rice, probably because of their early connections with the East, with its spice trade and magnificent galleons. Rice is cooked with different vegetables, or meat and poultry. Among rice dishes, *risi e bisi* is the one immediately associated with hazy canals and flaky stuccoed walls. This is the dish that opened the banquet given by the Doges in honour of St Mark, on the 25th of April every year, in the long passed era of the Republic of Venice.

The peas in the dish should be the first and earliest of the crop, extremely small and sweet. These are the kind of peas that we used to love eating raw when we were small.

The dish ideally should be quite moist, almost like a thick soup.

55g (2oz) butter
1 medium onion, skinned and sliced finely
675g (1½lb) peas in shells*
A large pinch nutmeg
750ml (1¼ pints) chicken stock *or* light meat stock
Salt
140g (5oz) thick Italian rice *or* yellow *Arborio* rice
3 tablespoons finely chopped parsley
55g (2oz) freshly grated Parmesan cheese
* *Frozen garden peas could be used, although far from ideal, in which case use 200g (7oz) and add them to the rice for the last 10 minutes of its cooking.*

In a large saucepan, melt the butter and sauté the onion until pale golden in colour. Take care not to overheat and brown the butter. Mix in the shelled peas and sauté for 2–3 minutes, stirring, adding the nutmeg towards the end. Pour in the stock and salt, cover and cook for 5 minutes. Add the rice and parsley, mix well, cover and simmer for about 30 minutes, stirring occasionally, until the rice is cooked but still a little firm. The dish should be very moist; if necessary add a few tablespoons of boiling water.

Finally, mix in the cheese and serve.

VEGETABLES
and Pasta
with Vegetables

Vegetarian or Not?

Despite the natural, religious and social restraints, Mediterraneans were determined to make the best of what was at their disposal: vegetables, olive oil, fish and occasionally a little meat. They had to improvise with combinations of ingredients, stretching their imaginations to achieve tempting and exciting dishes. But primarily they were open to suggestions; they observed and learned from each other through their historical contacts. The excitement, the short temper, the flamboyance that characterizes Mediterraneans, their hot-bloodedness in one over-simplified term, required intrigue and artistry in their dishes as in other aspects of their life. Vegetables, wild greens and fungi collected from the hillsides, and all kinds of pulses were prepared with devotion and cooked with extravagance; and each combination was viewed with wonder. As a result, some of the best vegetable dishes have originated in the area. What Mediterranean cuisine has done for vegetables is matched by no other cuisine in the world, apart perhaps from the Indian. Gone was the era of the boiled vegetable!

> The Spaniards, like the heroes in the Iliad, seldom
> boil their food (eggs excepted), at least not in water,
> for frying, after all, is but boiling in oil. (Richard
> Ford)

To the Mediterranean, a vegetable has no identity until it is on the table. An aubergine, for instance, is not an aubergine until it has been fried and combined with garlic, tomatoes and olive oil. Vegetables, therefore, were fried, stuffed with

101

other vegetables or with fruit and nuts, baked and aromatized with the fragrant herbs of the hillsides and, the foundation of all Mediterranean cooking, garlic.

> In this country [France], I was almost poisoned with garlic, which they mix in their ragouts and all their sauces; nay the smell of it perfumes the very chambers, as well as every person you approach.
> (Tobias Smollett)

Vegetables were otherwise casseroled in varying combinations, vividly enriched by the brilliant scarlet of the summer tomatoes; or sharpened and enlivened by their intimate fusion with that most male fruit of all, the golden lemon, fragrant but assertive and, when added in excess, uniquely domineering. Occasionally, vegetables were buried in the glowing ashes of primitive fires and then pulped and served with robust bread, or covered with cheese or eggs and baked; and always enriched by generous quantities of fragrant olive oil, according to the wealth of the respective household.

All in all, what was to become a deliberate and self-conscious movement, classified as 'vegetarianism' with the establishment of the English Vegetarian Society in 1847 in England, was a natural and unconscious way of life in the Mediterranean countries. One of the English Vegetarian Society's luminaries, H. S. Salt, in his *Flesh or Fruit*, an essay on food reform published in 1866, makes the pertinent comment that:

> The very existence of persons who abstain from flesh-food is to most Englishmen a cause of amusement and surprise; a vegetarian is a social anomaly worth looking at, and perhaps worth laughing at, whenever and wherever he may be encountered; the *anthropophagi* [cannibals] of old could hardly be regarded with more curiosity than the modern *akreophagists* [one who abstains from meat, from the Greek words, *kreas* = meat, and *phago* = eat].

This 'social anomaly' which Salt and his followers were attempting to encourage among the traditionally meat-eating northern Europeans (as has already been illustrated by the reactions of that flesh-eater Tobias Smollett in 1766), was the norm for Mediterraneans, for reasons of expediency, habit and, to some degree, preference as they had always been aware of the charms and advantages of vegetarian-based cuisine.

Of course, the Mediterranean is not strictly vegetarian, by Salt's definition. Meat is eaten with enthusiasm and so is fish. And, as an Arab friend reminded me, the occasional meat bone that may be available will be thrown into a casserole of beans or chickpeas, or a handful of minced meat into a pot of vegetables, without much hesitation. In the same way, the Spaniards will also add chunks of *chorizo* – a pork sausage containing amounts of fat, garlic and *pimentón* (see page 104) – or morsels of Catalonian *butifarra*, which is a kind of spiced cummin-scented pork sausage containing the blood of the animal. *Morcilla*, a spicy pork sausage with a distinctive smoky flavour, will also be added. The Italians will start a vegetable soup or casserole of pulses by frying a few slivers of *pancetta* (salted ham) or by adding a ham bone. The Arabs may throw a couple of sheeps' feet into a bubbling pot of otherwise fleshless ingredients.

What distinguishes Mediterranean cuisine, however, is its relatively restricted reliance on meat and its rich celebration and creative enjoyment of vegetables, with fleshless or nearly fleshless days regarded as normal.

Dishes that contain no meat or fish even have special names; in Spain they are called *viudos* – widowed or unpaired, for example *garbanzos viudos*. In Turkey such dishes are meant to be cooked with olive oil so they are called *zeydinyagli* – with oil, and in Greece the terminology is similar – *lathera*, with oil or oily.

Most of the vegetable, pulse or grain dishes in this book will provide a complete meal and if combined with one or two dishes from the appetizers or the salad section, as the prevailing Mediterranean custom calls for, the meal will be even more complete and enticing, e.g. serve *fagioli con tonno* (page 185) followed by *penne con zucchini* (page 142) or *tortilla Espagñola* (page 154). Alternatively, serve a grilled pepper salad (page 183) followed by pulses such as *garbanzos a la Catalana* (page 168), or the Greek soup *fasolatha* (page 93) or *melanzane ripiene* (page 117). The combinations are endless.

Pimentón
Spanish Paprika

Wonderful, bright scarlet peppers are always found in Spanish markets, and when dried and powdered they become the popular *pimentón* (paprika) called for in most Spanish recipes. This can be either *pimentón dulce* – sweet as the word suggests, or *pimentón picante* which is of the hotter, cayenne type.

Spanish people are particular about the source of origin of their *pimentón* and they tend to buy it in large quantities once a year from their preferred outlet (especially if they are making their own *chorizo* – very savoury sausages). The best peppers in Spain come from the *Rioja* country, Navarre and Old Castile, and consequently this is where the best *pimentón* will also be found and, needless to say, the best *chorizo*.

If travelling around the Navarre province in September you will be startled by the astounding spectacle of the bright scarlet peppers in *riestras* – threaded – hanging in unison from the balcony of each household against the white walls, alongside the golden bunches of corn, all drying in the sun.

My Spanish friend in London, Lala Isla, would only buy the *pimentón* of Aldea Nueva in Navarre, and had it sent here by one of her relatives. Imagine her dismay when I returned from Spain with a little tin of *pimentón* bought in Barcelona. There followed a very enlightening session, and beautiful samples of *her pimentón* followed posthaste from Navarre!

How To Prepare Globe Artichokes

There are many different kinds of artichokes, differing in colour, shape and size. The more highly regarded are the smaller, oval shaped, dark purple ones which are indeed delicious. On the Aegean island of Alonnisos, this is the sole variety grown so we consider ourselves fortunate when we are there in the spring. Then there are the green, oval ones, mostly grown in Greece, Turkey, North Africa and Italy, and lastly the large round ones that are grown in France and Spain. In Italy tiny, young artichokes are sold which have not developed an inner hairy choke and consequently need very little preparation. Also in Italy, particularly in Rome, artichokes are often sold in the markets already prepared.

In Peloponnisos, in Greece, there is still a wild variety which bears wicked thorns at the end of each petal or leaf. And on the island of Crete, they have a cultivated version which still bears the thorns but it is much larger and magnificently beautiful. Both these types have an exquisite taste. (If in Crete during the spring, seek them out, even if only to look at them. There is a wonderful market at Chania.)

Artichokes should be firm and brightly coloured, not droopy and brown at the edges. They discolour quickly so should be rubbed with lemon juice as soon as they are prepared and then dropped into acidulated water.

Cut the stems (but do not discard), leaving about 2.5cm (1in) attached on the artichoke, unless the recipe specifies to trim it at the base.

Bend the hard outer leaves of the artichoke backwards

105

and snap off at their base, until three-quarters or a little more have gone and the soft inner ones appear. Slice approximately 2.5cm (1in) off the conical top horizontally and discard it.

At this stage you have to remove the hairy 'choke' and the purple thorny leaves surrounding it. A simple way to do this, in case you are unfamiliar with artichoke 'anatomy', is to slice the artichoke in half, exposing the inner lining of the heart, and, using a stainless steel spoon or a small knife, just scrape away the 'choke' and discard. Once you get used to this you can leave the artichoke whole and perform the same cleaning task from the top collar of leaves. Pull out the purple, short, inner leaves first, then insert a small knife or spoon and scrape away the hairy 'choke', being careful not to scrape the heart, which is the real delicacy. Now, using a knife, trim the reserved stems of their outer hard, green skin, exposing the inner whitish flesh which is very tasty and can be eaten raw, added into salads or, of course, added in the casserole with the rest of the artichokes. Pare the hard green base of the leaves, exposing the smooth white surface inside.

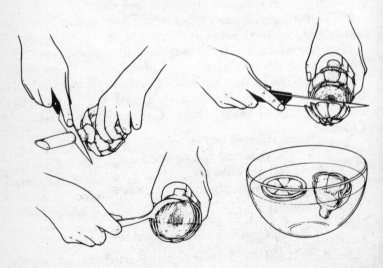

Artichauts à la Barigoule

Stuffed Globe Artichokes

FRANCE/PROVENCE

This recipe has been adapted from Ann Willan's *French Regional Cooking*, where she says the name *barigoule* is derived from the Provençal word for thyme, *farigoule*. Artichokes are, for me, the queen of garden vegetables, superior in taste and texture to everything else. The quantities below are for a first course or a light lunch, otherwise they should be doubled.

4 medium or large globe artichokes
Juice of ½ lemon

FILLING

4 tablespoons olive oil
1 medium onion, skinned and diced finely
110g (4oz) unsmoked bacon, diced finely
140g (5oz) firm mushrooms, wiped clean
2 cloves garlic, peeled and crushed
85g (3oz) fresh breadcrumbs
1 tablespoon fresh thyme, chopped *or* 1 teaspoon dried thyme
1 egg, lightly beaten

STOCK

1 onion, skinned and chopped
2 carrots, trimmed and chopped
120ml (4fl oz) olive oil
Salt and freshly ground black pepper
150ml (5fl oz) dry white wine
Chicken stock *or* water
1 teaspoon fresh thyme, chopped, *or* ½ teaspoon dried thyme

Prepare the artichokes whole as described on page 105, but trim their stalks to the base, in order to stand them upright, then put them in cold water to which has been added some lemon juice. Trim the stalks of their hard outer green surface and put in the bowl also.

Next, prepare the filling. In a saucepan, heat the olive oil and sauté the onion gently without browning it. Turn up the heat and sauté the bacon for 2 minutes, stirring once or twice. Add the mushrooms and cook in the same way until their moisture evaporates. Then mix in the garlic, breadcrumbs and herbs and remove from the heat. When the mixture is slightly cooler, pour in the beaten egg and mix well. Fill the artichokes with this mixture, pressing it down with your fingers, until they are well filled or rather piled up with the filling.

To make the stock, place the chopped onion, artichoke stalks and carrots in the bottom of a saucepan that will accommodate the artichokes closely and in one layer. Rest the artichokes on top, wedging them in. Pour the olive oil over them, add salt and pepper and pour in the wine. Add enough hot chicken stock or water to come halfway up the artichokes. Sprinkle the thyme on top, cover and cook slowly for about 40 minutes. Once or twice while they are cooking, tilt the saucepan and, using a spoon, moisten the artichokes with some of the juices.

Habas Verdes a la Granadina

Fresh Broad Beans with Globe Artichokes

SPAIN

1½kg (3lb) fresh broad beans, shelled
4 fresh globe artichoke hearts, prepared as
 described on page 105
150ml (5fl oz) olive oil
2 large onions, skinned and chopped finely
1 clove garlic, peeled and crushed
340g (12oz) tomatoes, peeled and chopped
2 tablespoons chopped parsley
2 bay leaves
1 teaspoon chopped fresh mint
Salt
½ teaspoon ground cummin
Large pinch saffron strands
1 teaspoon paprika
2 crustless slices of bread, fried in oil first and
 soaked in some water
1 egg per person

Shell the beans and set aside. Drop the prepared artichoke hearts in lightly salted boiling water, boil for 4–5 minutes and remove with a slotted spoon. Boil the shelled beans in the same saucepan for 6–8 minutes. Drain, reserving the water.

In a medium-sized saucepan, heat the olive oil and brown the onions and garlic, then add the tomatoes and fry a little longer. Add the beans, artichoke hearts, the herbs and enough of the reserved broth until they are almost covered; mix in the salt, cover and cook for 20 minutes until soft.

In the meantime, combine the cummin, saffron strands (there is no need to pre-soak them) and paprika in a bowl; add the soaked and shredded bread and mix to make a paste. Add this to the beans, mix well and cook, uncovered, for a further 5 minutes. Spread this into an oven dish, make four little wells and break an egg into each. Cook in a preheated oven, gas no. 4 (350°F/180°C), until the eggs are cooked to your taste.

The Exotic Aubergine

When one thinks of Mediterranean food, the associations brought to mind are inevitably summery: of dishes rich in colour, and of tastes that are accentuated by the sun and heat. And among the summer vegetable dishes, the one that most embodies the Mediterranean is that containing the exotic aubergine. Although not a Mediterranean native, but an Asian immigrant in a sense, it has come to epitomize a landmark in Mediterranean cooking, as it is the most versatile and appetizing of vegetables, and is aptly called the *sayyid al-Khudar*, or 'lord of vegetables', in the Arab-speaking world. Derived from the Sanskrit *vatin-ganah*, it went under the Arabic name *badhinjan*, which remained the root of all the subsequent European names: the Italian *melanzane*, the Greek *melitzana*, Spanish *berenjena*, French *aubergine*, etc. It is thought that the aubergine was introduced to the West by the Arabs in the Islamic period, as first mentions of it are found in Islamic manuscripts of the ninth century.

Late in December 825, frantic preparations for a lavish wedding were taking place in a village on the Tigris, south of Baghdad. The marriage, one of acute political importance among the intrigue-plotting Caliphs and Vezirs of the area, was to be between the powerful Caliph al-Mamun, son of Harun al-Rashid, and Khadijah, daughter of the Vezir al-Hasan ibn Sahl. Khadijah became better known under the pet-name of Buran, after a Persian princess of the seventh century. The actual event, which lasted over two weeks, has been deposited in history ablaze with splendour and mythical tales, such as that of the bridegroom being showered with one thousand pearls on his arrival.

Some 125 years later, dishes named after the bride began

to appear, even though there is no record of the dishes served at the magnificent wedding. In particular, a dish called *badhinjan Buran*, or Buran's aubergine, which in general called for small aubergines, sliced and soaked in salted water, then fried in a mixture of olive and sesame oil and finally sprinkled with various aromatics, such as pepper, rue and caraway. (Charles Perry, *Journal of Gastronomy*.) Was it, then, the sumptuous wedding of Buran that introduced aubergines to us and showed us the way to master their bitterness?

By the tenth century, aubergines also appeared on Byzantine tables, and although courgettes or marrows around the same period were regarded by the Byzantines as containing no nourishment, the aubergine with its exotic bitterness, *la curiosité* of the time, was higher up on the culinary ladder. However, it did not immediately become the much loved vegetable we know. It seems that its excessive bitterness was an obstacle that had to be overcome first. In the eleventh century, anecdotes are written about a Bedouin who compared the aubergine with *zaqqum*, which is the bitter tree of Hell; another Bedouin who was asked what he thought of the aubergine cooked by Buran, replied: 'Even if Maryam the mother of Jesus split it and Sarah the wife of Abraham cooked it and Fatimah the daughter of the Prophet served it, I would have no taste for it.' (Charles Perry)

Whatever the truth of the creation of the original *badhinjan Buran*, from it a whole range of aubergine dishes evolved.

From Professor Arberry's 'A Baghdad Cookery Book', we can trace a number of dishes such as *buran* – a splendid casserole of meat balls with aubergine purée on top; and *madfuna* – a casserole of meat and fried aubergines, which is still a popular dish in Turkey and Greece, and in Algeria and Morocco, where it is known as *braniya*. (See Rena Salaman, *Greek Food*, p. 291.)

Similarities with contemporary aubergine dishes are abundant; the Turkish delicacy of *hunkar beğendi* – the Sultan's delight – is almost identical to the thirteenth-century *buran*; aubergine pickles are made in an identical way to *badhinjan mukhallal*, in Turkey and all the Arab countries; and *madfuna* has contributed to the delightful variations of stuffed aubergines all over the Mediterranean.

Curiously enough, Professor Arberry's translation mentions not only *buraniyyah* but also *buraniyya al-qar* – a casserole made with gourd instead of aubergines, an indication that the famous name of Buran was being borrowed for dishes that might contain no aubergine at all. So, in Egypt and Syria *burani* is nowadays a dish made with every vegetable other than aubergines; in Spain, *boronia* or *moronia*, according to Charles Perry, is a ratatouille, and the most distinct and far-fetched version is the Turkish and Greek *burani* which no longer has any associations with aubergine and is really a glorified pilaf, and I do literally mean glorified as it is quite sumptuous; the recipe is on page 174.

Preparing Aubergines

All aubergines have to undergo an initial preparation in order to rid them of their bitterness; the only exception is the slim, light purple variety.

These first steps, and particularly the correct frying of the aubergines, are of great importance as the success of the whole dish depends on them. Frying them is a little tricky as they brown and burn almost instantly. Remember that aubergines are quite spiteful and that they need love and undivided attention; turn your back on them for a few seconds and they will immediately gain revenge by burning! It is best not to attempt to do anything else while frying aubergines. For this reason, I prefer to use two frying pans at the same time, in order to shorten the frying time overall. They should never be fried over too high a heat.

Top and tail the aubergines, wash them and slice according to the recipe, immerse them in a large bowl of salted water (about ¼ teaspoon salt). Place an inverted plate on top, with a weight, such as a tin, on it in order to keep the aubergines well immersed, and leave for 30 minutes.

Rinse the aubergines under running cold water, squeezing them gently to get rid of their brown bitter juices and the salt. Either place them in a colander, well spread out to give them room to drain, or spread them on a clean tea towel.

Frying Aubergines

Dry them in clean tea towels, otherwise they will spit when put into the hot oil. Preferably use two frying pans, the largest you have, and add quite a lot of oil, about 1cm (½in) up their sides. Heat the oil well before adding the aubergines, otherwise they will immediately absorb it.

Add a layer of aubergines in each frying pan and after 1 minute turn the heat down slightly so that they do not brown too quickly.

Allow them to fry over medium heat for about 2 minutes on each side until light golden. Take out and spread on absorbent kitchen towel to drain excess oil.

NEVER add oil to a frying pan which has aubergines in it, as they will absorb it instantly. If more oil is needed, add it before frying the next batch of aubergines and heat it properly first.

Buran

A Predecessor of the Turkish Hunkar Beğendi?

Take egg-plant, and boil lightly in water and salt, then take out and dry for an hour. Fry this in fresh sesame oil until cooked: peel, put into a dish or a large cup, and beat well with a ladle, until it becomes like *Kabis* (pulped).

Add a little salt and dry coriander. Take some Persian milk, mix in garlic, pour over the egg-plant and mix together well. Take red meat, mince fine, make into small *cabobs* (round hamburgers), and melting fresh oil, throw the meat into it, stirring until browned. Then cover with water and stew until that water has evaporated and only the oil remains. Pour on top of this the egg-plant, sprinkle with fine ground cummin and cinnamon and serve. (Professor A. J. Arberry, 'A Baghdad Cookery Book'.)

Hunkar Beğendi

Stumbling across the origins of a dish buried in the past is quite exciting. The sense of continuity, and social interaction – sometimes across borders – that this suggests, I find fascinating. This Turkish dish, which literally means 'His Majesty loves it', is an aubergine purée, served with either a meat or chicken casserole, or with marble-sized hamburgers in a sauce. However, during a recent International Food Congress in Turkey, we were served a dish at the Pera Palace Hotel, Istanbul, called *ali-nazik* which also bears perhaps even greater similarities to the above description. *Ali-nazik* consisted of a garlicky aubergine and yoghurt purée with a savoury minced meat served on top. Here is the recipe for *Hunkar Beğendi*.

1kg (2lb) large round aubergines
55g (2oz) butter
55g (2oz) plain flour
1 teaspoon ground cummin
425ml (15fl oz) warm milk
Salt and freshly ground black pepper

Rest the aubergines on a low gas flame and cook them for 20–30 minutes, turning regularly, until they are charred outside but soft inside, which will give them a special flavour. (Originally this would have been done by the most familiar cooking method of burying them in hot ashes, or over a slow charcoal fire.) Alternatively, prick them and grill them, turning regularly.

Once cooked, immerse them for 2 minutes in a bowl of cold water to which has been added a little salt. This will make them easier to peel and will extract their bitter juices. Peel them, squeeze them and leave in a colander for 30 minutes. Chop them with a knife until they look quite mashy, or put them through a food processor or blender briefly.

Melt the butter in a saucepan over gentle heat and add the flour gradually and the cummin, stirring constantly. Add the aubergine, mix well and gradually pour in the warm milk, stirring until the mixture is well blended. Season and beat with a small balloon whisk over gentle heat for 10 minutes, until the mixture thickens and the flour is cooked. Serve with either meat or chicken as above or with *tamia* (page 53).

Melanzane Parmigianae
Baked Aubergines with Tomatoes and Cheese

ITALY

In the crowded streets of Naples at lunchtime, one can almost follow the fragrant trail of scorched aubergines to the nearest *rosticceria*; and if you explore the winding back streets, with the jostling washing lines strung above your head, you are more than likely to sample the heartiest versions of *parmigiana*.

I first encountered it long ago in 1962. We drove into Naples after an early morning visit to Pompeii and, in the sparkling warmth of the March sunshine, Naples seemed like a riotous galleon assaulting the senses: the colours, the crowds, the confusion, the noise, the smells and the huge blackened trays of *parmigiana* and *pizza*, just emerging from the old-fashioned cavernous ovens, their sharp aromas impressing my youthful and innocent tastebuds.

Parmigiana is very much like a multiple sandwich, beginning and ending with fried aubergines and layered in between with tomatoes and cheese. If made in the summer when sugary tomatoes are available, it is best with chopped raw tomatoes; if the tomatoes are ripe and soft, they are best skinned first, then grated through the large side of a grater and drained of some of their liquid juices before being used. If canned tomatoes are used, it is best to make the cooked Neapolitan *pomarola* sauce (page 79).

If mozzarella cheese is not available, substitute with Bel Paese, but the most important ingredient is a rich Parmesan cheese.

> **1.2kg (2½lb) aubergines**
> **Salt**
> **150ml (5fl oz) vegetable oil, for frying**
> **1kg (2lb) tomatoes, skinned and chopped *or***
> **　1 portion *pomarola* sauce (see page 79)**
> **Freshly ground black pepper**
> **1 tablespoon dried oregano**
> **225g (8oz) mozzarella cheese, sliced and cubed**
> **85g (3oz) grated Parmesan cheese**
> **3 tablespoons olive oil**

Prepare the aubergines as described on page 112, slicing them lengthways. Fry them in the vegetable oil and drain on absorbent kitchen towel as described. It is vital to get rid of most of their oil so that the finished dish is not too heavy. Make the *pomarola* sauce, if using, following the recipe on page 79.

Choose a small roasting pan. A 26 x 26cm (10 x 10in) one that I use gives three layers of aubergines; a slightly smaller one would be even better. Line the bottom tightly with fried aubergines, and sprinkle over the chopped tomatoes or *pomarola* sauce, some black pepper, oregano, small pieces of mozzarella cheese and a generous sprinkling of Parmesan cheese. Continue in this fashion and finish with a layer of aubergines. Sprinkle some oregano and Parmesan cheese generously all over the top, dribble over the olive oil and cook in a preheated oven, gas no. 5 (375°F/190°C), for 45 minutes. The mixture should be quite dry after this time.

Remove from the oven and allow to stand for 10 minutes, as with all layered dishes, to enable it to settle and thus be easier to slice and serve.

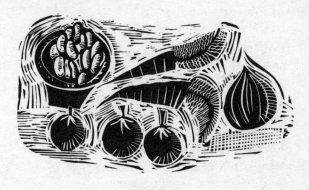

Melanzane Ripiene
Stuffed Aubergines

ITALY/FRANCE

Once the connection of aubergines with Mediterranean cooking has been made, the dishes that come to mind inevitably bear a profuse garlic aroma and are splashed with the scarlet of that other immigrant to the Mediterranean, the tomato. Aubergines have also been combined with a multitude of other ingredients such as rice, meat, nuts, eggs, cheese, and yoghurt; but salted anchovies are not one of the ingredients normally associated with aubergines.

Nevertheless, *Melanzane Ripiene* is one of the most interesting aubergine dishes and deserves more attention. It originated in Sicily and it is also found in the South of France. In Italy, salted anchovies, which have been rinsed and soaked in water first, are used, but these are almost impossible to find in Britain. They can be substituted with canned anchovies strained from their oil.

Serves 6

3 aubergines, about 1kg (2lb), trimmed and sliced in half lengthways
90ml (3fl oz) vegetable oil, for frying

STUFFING

140g (5oz) fresh breadcrumbs
60ml (2fl oz) olive oil
2 cloves garlic, peeled and crushed
8 anchovy fillets, roughly chopped
10 black olives, stoned and chopped
2 tablespoons chopped parsley
1 teaspoon each dried oregano and thyme
Freshly ground black pepper

Immerse the aubergines in salted water as described on page 112. Drain them and pat dry, then scoop out some of their flesh, about one third, leaving boat-shaped halves. Chop the extracted flesh finely and set aside.

In a frying pan, heat the vegetable oil and shallow-fry the aubergines on both sides. Take them out of the frying pan and place them side by side in a baking dish.

Prepare the stuffing, using a clean frying pan. First reserve two tablespoons of the breadcrumbs. Heat the olive oil gently, add the garlic and stir until aromatic, without browning; stir in the aubergine flesh and sauté for about 6–8 minutes, gradually adding 4 tablespoons of water and stirring occasionally; add all the remaining ingredients and cook for a further 2–3 minutes.

Fill the aubergine halves with this mixture, sprinkle the reserved breadcrumbs on top and add 5 tablespoons water to the dish. Bake in a preheated oven, gas no. 3 (325°F/160°C), for 30 minutes. Like most aubergine dishes, this can be served hot or at room temperature.

Bringiel Agrodolce
Aubergines in Sweet-and-Sour Sauce

MALTA

A Maltese dish with a definite flavour of pre-Islamic Persian cuisine about it. Sweet-and-sour dishes found their way along the North African coast and into Europe during the Arab invasions of the seventh and eighth centuries; a kind of Muslim 'Crusades' from East to West. Similar dishes are found in Sicily, Spain and the Arab countries.

> 675g (1½lb) aubergines, trimmed, washed and cubed
> 6 tablespoons olive oil
> 4 cloves garlic, peeled but left whole
> 340g (12oz) tomatoes, peeled and chopped, *or* 1 large 396g (14oz) can without the liquid, chopped
> 3—4 tablespoons chopped fresh mint, *or* 1 teaspoon dried mint
> Salt and freshly ground black pepper
> 1 teaspoon sugar
> 2 teaspoons wine vinegar

Immerse the aubergines in salted water as described on page 112. Drain them in a colander.

In a large frying pan or casserole, heat the olive oil and sauté the garlic, remove and reserve. Dry the aubergine cubes in a clean tea towel, add them to the olive oil and fry briskly, stirring to prevent them from sticking. Add the chopped tomatoes, mint, salt, pepper and garlic, cover and simmer for 20 minutes, stirring occasionally. Then add the sugar and vinegar, stir and cook for a further 5 minutes. It is best to let the dish stand for a few hours, or overnight, in order to blend the sweet and sour flavours. It also tastes best served at room temperature.

Italian Aubergines

ITALY

A rather special but fiddly dish with a rich and delicious taste. Cook the aubergines in advance, perhaps the previous day, and you can then enjoy the dish rather than despairing of the time taken to make it.

> 675g (1½lb) large aubergines, trimmed and washed
> 90ml (3fl oz) vegetable oil
> Salt and freshly ground black pepper
> ½ portion *pomarola* sauce (see page 79)
> 110g (4oz) Italian *prosciutto or* ham, thinly sliced
> 110g (4oz) Swiss Gruyère, Emmenthal *or* Jarlsberg
>   cheese, cubed
> 55g (2oz) grated Parmesan cheese
> Some fresh basil, finely chopped

Slice the aubergines lengthways in 0.6cm (¼in) thick slices and immerse them in salted water for 30 minutes, then dry them, as described on page 112.

In a frying pan, heat the vegetable oil and fry them briefly until pale golden in colour, then drain on absorbent kitchen towel and season them.

Prepare the *pomarola* sauce, following the recipe on page 79.

When cool enough to handle, place the aubergine slices on a chopping board, line each one with a slice of *prosciutto* and a sprinkling of the cubed cheese in the middle and fold the two narrow edges over each other, like a cigar; secure with a toothpick. Lightly oil a pretty oven dish, such as a quiche dish, and arrange them carefully, folded edges uppermost. Spoon the tomato sauce thinly over the aubergines, sprinkle the Parmesan cheese over and bake in a preheated oven, gas no. 4 (350°F/180°C), for 30 minutes. Sprinkle the basil over and serve.

Ratatouille

Courgette and Aubergine Casserole

FRANCE/PROVENCE

A book on Mediterranean vegetables could not be complete without the ubiquitous ratatouille. So, here it is. The result should be a far from watery concoction, and it should have a definite garden aroma, either from fresh or dried herbs.

450g (1lb) aubergines, trimmed, washed and sliced
   in 2.5cm (1in) circles
120ml (4fl oz) olive oil
1 medium onion, skinned and chopped finely
2 cloves garlic, peeled and crushed
675g (1½lb) courgettes, trimmed, washed and
   scraped lightly
1 green or red pepper, cored, de-seeded and sliced
450g (1lb) tomatoes, peeled and chopped
1 tablespoon each of chopped fresh thyme and
   marjoram *or* 1 teaspoon each dried
Salt and freshly ground black pepper
2 tablespoons finely chopped parsley

Immerse the aubergines in salted water for 30 minutes as described on page 112. Drain and cube.

In a heavy casserole, heat the olive oil and sauté the onions, until glistening. Dry the aubergines on a clean tea towel and add to the pan. Fry together, stirring continuously, rather fiercely for 2 minutes, then turn down the heat, add the garlic and fry briefly until aromatic. Stir in the courgettes and pepper and, once they are coated in the oil, add the tomatoes, herbs and seasoning. Cover and simmer for 20 minutes, avoiding adding any water unless necessary. Stir in the parsley and cook for a further 5 minutes.

Ratatouille can be served hot or at room temperature, and it tastes better when cooked in advance.

Calabacines al Horno
Courgettes Baked with Garlic

SPAIN

This has certain similarities to the French *gratin de courgettes*, where the lightly parboiled courgettes are covered with a thin layer of béchamel sauce, dusted with cheese and breadcrumbs and then baked.

> 1kg (2lb) courgettes, trimmed, washed and scraped lightly
> 2 cloves garlic, crushed
> 6 tablespoons olive oil
> 55g (2oz) fresh breadcrumbs
> 2 tablespoons finely chopped parsley
> Salt and freshly ground black pepper
> Juice of ½ lemon

Cook the courgettes in lightly salted boiling water for 8 minutes and drain. Cut them in half lengthways and arrange them, in one layer, side by side, in a suitably-sized oven dish.

In a bowl, mix the garlic with the olive oil, breadcrumbs, parsley, salt and pepper and sprinkle over the courgettes. Finally, sprinkle the lemon juice over them and bake in a preheated oven, gas no. 4 (350°F/180°C), for 20 minutes until the top is crisp and golden.

Torta di Zucchini
Baked Courgettes with Mozzarella

ITALY

I must admit that I invented this dish, inspired by a similar potato recipe and a baked courgette dish that my mother used to make. The result is a delicious cross between the two, but always maintaining the Italian tradition. It is without a shade of doubt one of the best vegetable dishes I know.

1kg (2lb) courgettes, trimmed, washed and scraped
 lightly
5 tablespoons sunflower oil *or* vegetable oil
3 tablespoons olive oil
1 portion *pomarola* sauce (see page 79) *or* 1kg (2lb)
 fresh tomatoes
170g (6oz) mozzarella cheese *or* one of the little
 parcels
1 teaspoon dried herbs, *or* some fresh herbs with
 basil if possible
Salt and freshly ground black pepper

Dry the courgettes in a clean tea towel and cut them thinly into rounds. In a large frying pan, heat the sunflower or vegetable oil and olive oil and fry the courgettes briskly but lightly, stirring, without being too meticulous about it. Remove them with a slotted spoon and drain on absorbent kitchen towel to soak up excess oil.

Prepare the *pomarola* sauce, following the recipe on page 79.

Spread the courgettes into a medium-sized ovenproof dish, preferably earthenware and of a light colour in order to show off the colour of the dish; season them, spread the tomato sauce over the top or, if using fresh tomatoes, trim them, slice thinly and spread over the courgettes, to cover the surface. Add the thinly sliced mozzarella cheese all over the top and bake in a preheated oven, gas no. 5 (375°F/190°C), for 30 minutes or until the mozzarella starts to melt and turn light golden.

Frigo di Patate, Cipolle e Zucchini
Baked Potatoes with Courgettes and Onions

ITALY

This recipe has been adapted from Wilma Pezzini's *Tuscan Cookbook*. It resembled the Greek *briami*, so familiar to me, but I felt it had more *brio*, so I could not resist including it. In the Greek version, the ingredients are simply mixed together raw and baked, while in this more interesting version they are lightly fried first.

450g (1lb) courgettes, trimmed, washed and scraped lightly
450g (1lb) potatoes, peeled and sliced thickly
90ml (3fl oz) olive oil
1 large onion, skinned and sliced thinly
Salt and freshly ground black pepper
Some fresh basil *or* a pinch of dried basil
½ portion *pomarola* sauce (see page 79)

Dry the courgettes, slice them into 5cm (2in) pieces and quarter them lengthways. Rinse and strain the potatoes.

In a large frying pan, heat the olive oil and sauté the courgettes, until they start to change colour. Remove with a slotted spoon into a medium-sized, oiled, ovenproof dish.

In the same pan, sauté the onions until they become transparent; add the potatoes and fry for approximately 10 minutes. Add to the courgettes with some seasoning and the basil, mix well and spread evenly.

Make the *pomarola* sauce, following the recipe on page 79. Pour the *pomarola* sauce over the mixture and bake in a preheated oven, gas no. 4 (350°F/180°C), for 40 minutes.

VARIATIONS

Sprinkle 85g (3oz) of freshly grated Parmesan cheese instead of *pomarola* sauce on top and bake as previously.

Place thin slices of tomatoes all over the top instead of the *pomarola* sauce and bake as previously.

Patates Antinaktes or Spastes

Potatoes with Coriander and Wine

This unusual dish takes its name from tossing (*antinasso* – to toss) the potatoes in the casserole, instead of stirring them, or from 'cracking' the potatoes before cooking them. It is not only unusual but extremely tasty, particularly when it is made with small, sweet Cyprus potatoes.

> 1kg (2lb) smallish potatoes
> 300ml (10fl oz) corn oil *or* sunflower oil
> 2 tablespoons coriander seeds, picked clean and
>   crushed roughly
> Salt and freshly ground black pepper
> 120ml (4fl oz) dry red wine

Wash the potatoes thoroughly, scrubbing them with a brush under running water. Place a few at a time on a marble or stone surface and hit each in the centre with a pestle to crack it, but it should remain in one piece. (Do not give up at this stage as it is worthwhile.) Dry them, then deep-fry them in the hot corn or sunflower oil, until light golden, then drain.

In a saucepan, gently heat 3 tablespoons of the corn or sunflower oil, add the coriander seeds, the potatoes, seasoning and pour the wine over them. Cover the saucepan and, holding the cover down, toss its ingredients a few times, in order to mix them. Cook gently for 4–5 minutes and repeat the tossing-and-return-to-the-heat method 3 more times until the potatoes are cooked, about 20 minutes in all.

Batata Bil Limoun
Potatoe and Lemon Casserole

MOROCCO

An appealing and unusual potato dish very similar to the Greek *patates lemonates*. Serve with plain yoghurt or *caçik* and a crisp green salad containing different kinds of leaves.

150ml (5fl oz) olive oil
2 medium onions, skinned and sliced finely
2 cloves garlic, peeled and crushed
1 tablespoon ground cummin
1 teaspoon ground coriander
$\frac{1}{4}$ teaspoon cayenne pepper
1kg (2lb) potatoes, peeled, and sliced thickly
Juice of $1\frac{1}{2}$ lemons
300ml (10fl oz) water
Salt
2 tablespoons chopped parsley

In a saucepan, heat the olive oil and sauté the onion until it glistens, then add the garlic and stir for a few seconds only, until aromatic. Mix in the spices, and stir for 1 minute, then add the potatoes and coat them in the oil. Pour the lemon juice and water over, add the salt, cover and cook for 20–30 minutes, making sure they do not stick. Sprinkle the parsley over and serve either hot or at room temperature.

Stuffat Tal-Pastard
Cauliflower Casserole

MALTA

Maltese cuisine, although true to its Mediterranean roots, presents a different face from its relatives, with brave but confident additions. The strong Arab influences are here more evident than anywhere else; the mixtures of sweet and sour, the raisins, the pine nuts, mixed with olives or salted anchovies. Similar cauliflower casseroles, without the raisins and the olives, are made in Greece, in Egypt, and in Turkey, but this is an interesting variation.

> 1 medium cauliflower, trimmed, washed and cut
>   into large florets
> 2 eggs, beaten lightly
> 55g (2oz) plain flour
> 150ml (5fl oz) or more vegetable oil for deep-frying
> 5 tablespoons olive oil
> 1 medium onion, skinned and sliced finely
> 2 tablespoons tomato purée diluted in 300ml
>   (10fl oz) hot water
> 2 tablespoons raisins, rinsed and drained
> 12 black olives
> Salt and freshly ground black pepper

Put the cauliflower into lightly salted boiling water, bring back to the boil and boil for 4 minutes then drain. Dip the cauliflower into the egg, then flour it lightly and deep fry in the hot vegetable oil, in batches, until pale golden.

Meanwhile, in a large saucepan, heat the olive oil and sauté the onion until transparent; add the diluted tomato purée and bring to the boil. Add the cauliflower and all the remaining ingredients, stir to coat in the sauce, cover and cook for about 15 minutes until quite tender.

VARIATION

I like adding other vegetables to this casserole in order to make it more substantial and give it more flavours. I also like adding a dried lime, a Persian habit, which makes it more tangy and gives at least an extra layer of taste and aroma to the dish.

You can add 2–3 courgettes, 2 carrots, 1–2 potatoes, 1 leek, all properly trimmed, washed and quartered into 2.5cm (1in) sticks. Add them to the onion as it becomes transparent and sauté together, stirring them for about 3 more minutes. Add the tomato purée diluted as before, the dried lime, cover and cook for 5 minutes before adding the cauliflower and remaining ingredients as in the above recipe.

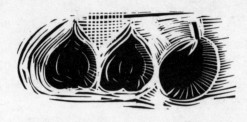

Cavolfiore alla Siciliana
Sicilian Cauliflower

ITALY

An unusual and assertive way in which to cook cauliflower, this produces the most unexpected crunchy results. This is an earthy, bold dish that instantly dispels the myth that cauliflower is boring.

> 1 cauliflower, trimmed and divided into florets
> 5 tablespoons olive oil
> 2 garlic cloves, peeled and crushed
> 6—8 anchovy fillets, chopped
> Freshly ground black pepper

Put the cauliflower into boiling salted water, bring back to the boil and cook for 3–4 minutes. Do not overcook; it should still be quite hard. Drain. In a saucepan, heat the olive oil and add the crushed garlic, stirring over low heat to prevent

129

it turning brown. Shortly after, add the chopped anchovies and stir for a few minutes until well amalgamated into a thick, pasty sauce. Stir in the cauliflower and lots of freshly ground pepper; fry briskly, coating it in the sauce, for 2–3 minutes, then serve.

Judias Verdes a la Castellana
Green Beans in the Castile Style

SPAIN

An interesting and unusual combination from Castile where, among other things, sweet peppers abound so they are used a lot in local cooking.

Serves 4—6

1kg (2lb) green bobby beans *or* French beans
4 green peppers, washed
6 tablespoons olive oil
3 cloves garlic, chopped finely
1 teaspoon *pimentón* (see page 104) *or* paprika
Salt
2 tablespoons chopped parsley

Top and tail the beans and string if necessary. Wash and drain them, then slice each in half. Cook them in lightly salted boiling water for 4–5 minutes until tender, then drain. Grill the peppers, turning them often, until they blister and blacken. When cool, peel them, discarding core and pips, and cut them into strips.

In a frying pan, heat the olive oil and sauté the garlic. Add the *pimentón* or paprika, stir briefly and add the peppers and the drained green beans. Adjust the seasoning, mix and cook for a further 3–4 minutes. Sprinkle with parsley and serve either hot or at room temperature.

130

Taze Fasulye

Green Bean Casserole

Bean casseroles are very popular all over the Middle East and Greece. Bobby beans and French beans are both excellent for this dish and they do not need stringing.

> 675g (1½lb) fresh beans, topped and tailed
> 8 tablespoons vegetable oil
> 1 medium onion, skinned and sliced finely
> 2 cloves garlic, peeled and sliced finely
> 2 medium potatoes, peeled, washed and sliced
> 450g (1lb) fresh tomatoes, peeled and chopped *or*
>   396g (14oz) can of tomatoes, chopped
> 150ml (5fl oz) hot water
> Salt and freshly ground black pepper

Cut the beans in half if too long, wash and drain them.

In a saucepan, heat the vegetable oil and fry the onion and garlic until pale golden in colour, then add the beans and potatoes and stir for 2–3 minutes until well coated in the oil. Add the fresh tomatoes and the water, or the canned tomatoes and half the amount of water, seasoning, and mix well. Cover and cook for 30 minutes until the vegetables are quite tender. Serve either hot or at room temperature.

Piselli Alla Romana

Fresh Pea Casserole with Parma Ham

'And the peas! No, I don't care about English peas. Too large and too lively for me ... I shall never forget my first experience of them,' he went on, laughing.

'There were two or three in the dish; just two or three; filled it up nicely. Looked like cannon-balls. What do they expect me to do with these things? I wondered. I didn't like to ask the waiter. One doesn't care to be taken for an ignorant stranger. Well, I landed one on my plate and began carving at it, to see if there was anything eatable inside the shell, when the durned thing slipped away from my knife and crashed on to the floor. Bounced up like a marble. I called for a nutcracker – "I shall want the largest you've got," I said. They couldn't find one. Now I'm not the sort of man, Mr Heard, to be beaten by a vegetable, if it really was a vegetable. Because, you see, it behaved more like a blamed mineral. I sent for the head waiter, and took him into my confidence. I tried to talk English, like I'm talking to you.

"What d'ye call these things?" I asked.

"Marrowfats, Sir."

"Ah, I thought they weren't peas. You've got *petits pois* down on the bill of fare. Better get that put right.

And now, how d'ye eat them?" "You bite them, Sir."

"What's that?" "You just bite them!" That's what he said.

"You bite them." Of course I didn't believe him. I thought it was just a bit of English humour...'
(Norman Douglas, *South Wind*.)

My first experience of peas in England was no less complicated than the above. Standing puzzled among the many canned varieties in a supermarket, trying to decode the instructions of a recipe handed over by a friend, was a cultural experience. Up to then, peas to me had been the green pods one buys in a market in the spring. A pea is a pea, is a pea. How could these be different? I thought. Well, I was destined to find out later on that evening when I had to pick and discard, one by one, the decadent, chemically aromatized, greying stone bullets from the grains of the pilaf. Almost twenty years later, mercifully things have improved.

The Romans need have no such fears! They are proud of the peas growing in the countryside around Rome as they are famed to be among the sweetest. And they are obviously harvested long before they have reached their mid-life crisis, unlike fresh English peas.

Piselli alla Fiorentina (Florence) is very similar to the Roman version.

1kg (2lb) fresh unshelled peas
3 tablespoons olive oil
30g (1oz) butter
1 medium onion, skinned and sliced finely
55g (2oz) unsmoked bacon, diced *or pancetta*
1 tablespoon chopped parsley
Freshly ground black pepper
90ml (3fl oz) hot water

Shell and wash the peas. In a saucepan, heat the olive oil and butter and sauté the onion until it glistens, then add the bacon and sauté for 2–3 minutes. Mix in the peas, parsley and seasoning and coat in the oil. Pour in the water, cover and cook for about 20 minutes or until the peas are tender. The Romans often use *prosciutto* which they simply cut in strips and add at the end of the cooking, instead of the bacon equivalent, the *pancetta*.

Bamia
Okra and Tomato Casserole

EGYPT

Okra is the aristocrat among vegetables in the eastern Mediterranean. Casseroles very similar to this one are cooked by Greeks and Turks. Okra is a fragile vegetable and consequently has to be treated gently.

133

1kg (2lb) okra
120ml (4fl oz) good quality vegetable oil
1 large onion, skinned and sliced finely
2 cloves garlic, peeled and chopped finely
2 teaspoons ground coriander
450g (1lb) fresh tomatoes, peeled and chopped, *or*
    396g (14oz) can, chopped
150ml (5fl oz) water
¼ teaspoon sugar
Salt and freshly ground black pepper

Peel the conical heads of the okra in a circular fashion, but avoid peeling them too deeply as this would release their glutinous contents. Drop the okra in a bowl of cold water, wash gently and drain in a colander. Repeat if needed.

In a saucepan, heat the vegetable oil and brown the onion lightly, add the garlic and sauté until aromatic; then stir in the coriander. Mix in the tomatoes and all the remaining ingredients, bring to the boil, add the okra and spread evenly through the sauce. Shake and rotate the saucepan rather than stirring, which might bruise and damage the okra. Cover and cook gently for 30–40 minutes.

Fave Alla Romana
Broad Beans Casserole

ITALY

Casseroles with broad beans are made all over the Mediterranean in the spring, as they start to appear in late March or April. In Malta they are combined with peas and lettuce in *hass, ful u pizelli*. Often they are combined with globe artichokes as they seem to have an affinity with them. *Zeytinyagli bakla* – broad beans cooked in olive oil (page 136) – from Turkey is almost identical to this Roman dish but of course without the *pancetta*, as is the Greek *koukia lathera*.

Moreover, there are the versions with artichokes, like the Turkish *zeytinyagli enginar* and the Greek *koukia me anginares*. All are absolutely enticing with a wonderful fresh garden taste.

Early last April we brought back the youngest and freshest pods (which I used whole, having peeled their strings first), purchased in the beautiful San José market off the *Ramblas* in Barcelona. When they are that small they are very sweet and the beans, once shelled, can be eaten raw, as we loved to consume them when we were small. Often they are offered in this manner in Italy.

> 1.5kg (3lb) fresh broad beans
> 90ml (3fl oz) olive oil
> 1 medium onion, skinned and sliced finely
> 140g (5oz) *pancetta*, cubed *or* unsmoked bacon
> Salt and freshly ground black pepper
> 600ml (1 pint) water
> 3 tablespoons finely chopped fresh dill *or* parsley

Shell the beans, keeping the young and tender pods intact but stringing both sides. Put them in a bowl of water, wash and drain them.

In a saucepan, heat the olive oil and sauté the onion until it becomes transparent, then add the *pancetta* and sauté for a further 2 minutes, stirring. Add the seasoning and water, then the broad beans and stir to coat them in the liquid. Cover and cook for about 50 minutes until the beans and pods are quite tender. The beans should have a thick, oily sauce by this time. Sprinkle the fresh, chopped herbs over and serve.

Zeytinyagli Bakla
Fresh Broad Beans with Yoghurt Sauce

TURKEY

This is a recipe that my mother's family cooked regularly in Istanbul, particularly during Lent when everybody was fasting and when the bright green pods are at their sweetest.

Choose smaller pods so that you can use them whole, as a lot of their flavour and aroma is in their skins. On the island of Alonnisos we are extremely fortunate, as there are whole fields of them and we can use only the aristocrats of the crop, which are the smallest and juiciest. The ideal compromise is to keep at least half of the quantity whole and peel the rest.

Served with fresh bread, this is a meal in itself, or it could be served as an appetizer.

> 1.5kg (3lb) fresh broad beans
> 150ml (5fl oz) olive oil
> 5—6 spring onions, chopped
> Juice of 1 lemon
> Salt
> 600ml (1 pint) cold water
> 4 tablespoons chopped fresh dill *or* 2 teaspoons
>   dried dillweed
>
> **SAUCE**
>
> 225g (8oz) natural yoghurt
> 2 cloves garlic, peeled and crushed
> Salt

Shell the large broad bean pods but keep the small and tender ones whole. String these by cutting all around with a sharp knife. Slice them into 5cm (2in) pieces and drop them in a bowl of cold water. Wash and drain them.

In a saucepan, heat the olive oil and sauté the onions until

136

pale golden in colour. Add the beans and sauté for a further few minutes. Pour over the lemon juice, add salt and the water, bring up to the boil, cover and simmer for 50–60 minutes, adding the dill towards the end. Turn out onto a platter and cool slightly before adding the sauce, but do not put in the refrigerator.

To make the sauce, beat the yoghurt with the garlic and salt, and spread over the beans. Sprinkle a little dill on top.

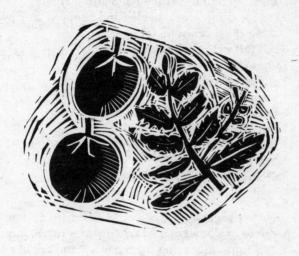

Turlu-Turlu
Mixed Vegetable Casserole

TURKEY

The name of this dish implies a hotch-potch, but a summer one. Courgettes, aubergines, sweet peppers, green beans and occasionally okra are all participants in the colourful parade.

Serve as a main course with *caçik* or plain yoghurt, or with *taramosalata*, black olives and *feta* cheese.

137

Serves 4—6

450g (1lb) aubergines, trimmed and cubed
450g (1lb) courgettes, trimmed, washed, scraped
lightly and cubed
170g (6oz) French beans, trimmed and sliced into
2—3 pieces
2 sweet peppers, green or red, cored, de-seeded and
cut in strips
1 potato, peeled and chopped
1 medium onion, skinned and sliced finely
225g (8oz) tomatoes, peeled and chopped *or* a small
225g (8oz) can tomatoes
60ml (2fl oz) vegetable oil
150ml (5fl oz) olive oil
3 cloves garlic, peeled and sliced finely
1 teaspoon oregano
1 tablespoon fresh chopped mint
2 tablespoons chopped parsley
1 tablespoon tomato paste diluted in 150ml (5fl oz)
hot water
Salt and freshly ground black pepper

Prepare all the vegetables, wash and drain them. Immerse
the aubergines in a bowl of cold salted water for 30 minutes.
Remove and rinse, squeezing them gently, and dry in a clean
tea towel.

In a frying pan, heat the vegetable oil and briskly fry the
aubergines (following the instructions on page 113), stirring
continuously, until pale golden in colour. Take out, drain
on absorbent kitchen towel and reserve. Heat the olive oil
in a saucepan and lightly brown the onions and garlic. Add
all the remaining vegetables, except the aubergines and
tomatoes, and sauté together for 5-6 minutes. Then add
the aubergines, tomatoes, herbs, tomato paste and seasoning,
mix and spread into a roasting tin. Cook in a preheated oven,
gas no. 5 (375°F/190°C), for 1½ hours, stirring occasionally
and adding a little water if needed.

Espinacas a la Catalana

Catalonian Spinach with Pine Kernels and Raisins

SPAIN

The Arab influence on Spanish, and particularly Catalonian, cooking is self-evident in this dish. This is a wonderfully unusual way in which to treat spinach. Claudia Roden cooked us a delicious dish of fried courgettes in a very similar fashion, a few years ago.

1kg (2lb) fresh spinach, trimmed
5 tablespoons olive oil
2 cloves garlic, peeled and chopped
55g (2oz) raisins
45g (1½oz) pine kernels, toasted first
1 tablespoon tomato paste, diluted in 2 tablespoons
    hot water (optional)
A little freshly grated nutmeg
Salt and freshly ground black pepper

Wash the spinach meticulously until no trace of grit remains, then drain it. Place the spinach in a large saucepan, add a little water and some salt, bring to the boil and cook for 3 minutes. Drain and rinse under cold water to retain its bright colour. Squeeze the spinach gently and chop roughly.

In a frying pan, heat the olive oil and sauté the garlic; add the remaining ingredients and stir for 1 minute. Add the spinach and fry briefly, stirring. Cover and cook for a further 5 minutes. Serve with fried croutons.

PASTA WITH VEGETABLES
Melanzane e Lasagne Alla Siciliana
Baked Pasta with Aubergines

ITALY

Aubergines and pasta are often combined in Italian cuisine and, although an inexpensive combination, the results are extremely tasty, as in this Sicilian dish.

> **2 aubergines, about 675g (1½lb)**
> **120ml (4fl oz) vegetable oil**
> **225g (8oz) lasagne**
> **1 portion *pomarola* sauce (see page 79)**
> **85g (3oz) freshly grated Parmesan cheese**
> **Salt and freshly ground black pepper**

Slice the aubergines lengthways and prepare as described on page 112. In a frying pan, heat the vegetable oil and fry the aubergines, then drain them on absorbent kitchen towel. Dribble a little oil into a large pan of salted, boiling water and cook the lasagne, in 2 or 3 batches to prevent them sticking, uncovered for 8–10 minutes. When cooked, drain them and spread the sheets out on a clean tea towel. Set aside.

Prepare the *pomarola* sauce, following the recipe on page 79.

Cover the base of a medium-sized oven dish with the aubergines and a layer of lasagne on top. Spread some of the *pomarola* sauce over, and sprinkle on plenty of Parmesan cheese and black pepper. Continue alternating the layers in the same way, finishing with a layer of *pomarola* sauce and plenty of cheese on top. Cook in a preheated oven, gas no. 5 (375°F/190°C), for 30 minutes. Serve with a crisp, green salad.

Cannelloni with Spinach and Ricotta
ITALY

This is a delicious dish, although a little time consuming. If one chooses the ready-made *cannelloni*, which does not need any preparatory cooking, then it becomes simpler. Alternatively the square pasta for lasagna can be used, particularly if bought freshly made. This should be boiled in lightly salted water for 5–6 minutes first.

Serves 6

225g (8oz) fresh spinach, trimmed
4 tablespoons olive oil
1 medium onion, skinned and sliced finely
55g (2oz) butter
110g (4oz) firm mushrooms, washed, dried and
   diced
A little grated nutmeg
Salt
170g (6oz) ricotta cheese
55g (2oz) freshly grated Parmesan cheese
1 egg
250g (9oz) packet *cannelloni all uovo*
30g (1oz) butter for the oven dish
½ portion *pomarola* sauce (see page 79)
1 portion béchamel sauce (see page 78)
55g (2oz) freshly grated Parmesan cheese

Wash the spinach meticulously until no trace of grit remains and drain it. Put it in a large saucepan with no additional water, cover and cook for about 8 minutes, stirring occasionally. Drain it and chop roughly.

In a saucepan, heat the olive oil and sauté the onion until it starts to change colour; add half the butter and, when it has melted, the mushrooms and sauté rather fiercely and briefly, until their liquid has evaporated. Add the spinach, nutmeg and salt and mix well. Cook for a further 2–3 minutes.

141

Empty into a bowl, cool slightly, mix with the cheeses and the egg and fill each *cannellone* using a tiny spoon and a chopstick to push the filling down. Place the filled *cannelloni* in a buttered oven dish.

Prepare the *pomarola* sauce and the béchamel sauce. Mix the two sauces together and spread evenly over the *cannelloni*, covering the whole surface. Sprinkle the cheese on top and dot with the remaining butter. Cook in a preheated oven, gas no. 5 (375°F/190°C), for 30 minutes, until crisp and golden on top.

Penne Con Zucchini
Pasta with Courgette Sauce

ITALY

Unusual but extremely tasty, this dish can be served at room temperature, which makes it the ideal candidate for a summer lunch *al fresco*.

If fresh basil is not available, substitute with any fresh, fragrant herbs you can find.

> 450g (1lb) courgettes, trimmed, washed and
>   scraped lightly
> 4 tablespoons olive oil
> Salt and freshly ground black pepper
> 4 tablespoons single cream
> 225g (8oz) *penne or penne rigate*
> 2 tablespoons finely chopped basil (see above) plus
>   a few whole basil leaves to garnish

Dry the courgettes and slice thinly. In a frying pan, heat the olive oil and sauté the courgettes gently, without browning them, for about 15 minutes until soft. Season them, combine with the cream and blend in a food processor or blender, until perfectly smooth.

Cook the pasta, uncovered, in plenty of salted, boiling water until *al dente*, and drain; place it in a large, pretty bowl, add the courgette sauce, the chopped herbs and mix well. Garnish with a few whole basil leaves.

Spaghetti alla Puttanesca

ITALY

This tasty dish, notorious in origin as well as in name, is quick and easy to prepare. Apparently, unfaithful Neapolitan wives returning home late, having spent their afternoon in illicit circumstances, resorted to it as the solution to the family dinner. Try it – well, at least the dish!

    5 tablespoons olive oil
    2 cloves garlic, peeled and sliced finely
    6—8 anchovy fillets, chopped
    110g (4oz) stoned and halved black olives
    1 small chilli, de-seeded and chopped
    2 tablespoons drained capers
    450g (1lb) tomatoes peeled and chopped *or* 396g
       (14oz) can tomatoes, finely chopped
    Salt
    225 (8oz) spaghetti

In a saucepan, heat the olive oil and sauté the garlic and anchovies briefly, until aromatic. Mix in the olives, chilli and capers and stir for 1–2 minutes. Add the tomatoes and salt, cover and cook gently for 20 minutes, until thickened.

Boil the spaghetti, uncovered, in plenty of salted, boiling water until it is *al dente*; drain, mix with the sauce, toss and serve immediately.

143

Spaghetti con Salsa Cruda

Spaghetti with Raw Tomato Sauce

ITALY

This was the speciality of our Italian friend Guido and back in the early 1970s, he often prepared it for us as a quick dinner after a day on the beaches of the Aeolian island of Salina, near Sicily.

Considering the simplicity and deliciousness of the sauce, I am surprised that the dish is not better known and more commonly used. It is perfect in hot weather when made with sugary, ripe tomatoes.

Serves 4 as a main course, or 6 as a first course

675g (1½lb) large, ripe tomatoes
1 clove garlic, peeled and crushed
3—4 tablespoons olive oil
3 tablespoons fresh chopped basil
285g (10oz) spaghetti
Freshly ground black pepper

The easiest way to prepare the tomatoes (assuming they are ripe) is to peel and grate them coarsely, holding them from the stalk side. Place them in a bowl and, just before the sauce is to be served, mix with the remaining ingredients.

Boil the spaghetti, uncovered, in plenty of lightly salted water until cooked *al dente*; drain and toss with the sauce. Serve immediately.

Serve separately a bowl of freshly grated parmesan cheese for those who like it, but I personally prefer this dish on its own.

EGGS

On Eggs and Omelettes

The love of eggs is proverbial in the Mediterranean, as they add a definite savoury note to an otherwise frugal table.

The dishes range from the simply boiled eggs sprinkled with a little salt and cummin that are sold in the markets in Morocco, to the *hamine* eggs of Egypt which accompany the *ful medames* – dried, small, round broad beans – and the whole roasted eggs of Cyprus. Then there are the deliciously fresh eggs fried in olive oil of the Greek islands, and the elaborate omelettes, if they can be called that, containing all kinds of vegetables, found in the Middle East, North Africa and Spain. Also, the deliciously moist scrambled egg and tomato concoctions, such as the French *pipérade*, which are found all over the Mediterranean.

Unlike our familiar Western-type omelettes, gently folded over mushrooms, spinach, or cheese and still soft and trembly in the heart, most of the Mediterranean omelettes are hearty affairs, thick and substantial; a cross between a pie and an omelette. These include the Arab *eggah*, where the eggs are mixed with cooked vegetables, poultry or meat and then baked in the oven, the *tortilla española* – the Spanish omelette, and the *chakchouka* of North Africa. In between, one also discovers variations on the same theme from one country to the next. The various Greek dishes called *sfougato* (a recipe for a vegetable one is given on page 157) are typical of this tradition, as is the French *tian*.

When in the mood, one can improvise on ingredients, combine them with herbs or spices, mix them with lightly beaten eggs, and cook either in a frying pan, as for the Spanish *tortilla*, or in the oven, as for the Arab *eggah*. For instance,

147

the extra portions of ratatouille from page 121 can be made into a *sfougato* and served for lunch the following day. Moreover, you could add some ground cummin and fresh coriander leaves or chopped fresh mint for a North African flavour.

La Pipérade or Tunisian Chakchouka

Each of the Mediterranean peoples has their own version of this dish, with their own name, but the contents are almost identical. A simple dish almost thrown together straight from a peasant's patch of earth in his own back garden, combining the most common of his produce: the inevitable summer tomatoes that no household can live without, sweet, aromatic peppers, and the freshly laid eggs from skinny and undisciplined chickens.

Chakchouka in Tunisia, *menemen* in Turkey, most probably originating from the old town of Menemeni near Smyrna, *omeletta me domates* in Greece, and on the Ionian island of Corfu it goes under the very eccentric name of *strapatsatha*. In Italy it is referred to literally as *uova con pomidori*, and in Spain it is known as *piperrada*.

La Pipérade

In France it is widely known as *la pipérade*, deriving its name from one of the three main ingredients, the sweet peppers. *Pipérade*, although a typically regional dish from the Basque country, is widely known and very close to the core of French country life. In its typical form it is served on a platter surrounded by thin slices of Bayonne ham, which is similar to the Italian *prosciutto*.

The dish must be made with rich, sugary, summer tomatoes, vibrant peppers and a fruity, velvety olive oil, although in France they may use some kind of fat, either pork fat, goose dripping or butter.

It is moreover totally blissful when served, out of an old blackened frying pan, in the open air, under the shade of vines with a huge round head of strongly scented basil at hand. But, of course, one can eat it on a manicured lawn!

4 tablespoons olive oil
1 medium onion, skinned and chopped finely
2 medium peppers, red or green, de-seeded and cut
   in strips
675g (1½lb) fresh tomatoes, peeled (ideally) and
   chopped
1 teaspoon of mixed dried herbs, such as oregano
   and thyme *or*, even better, fresh basil, chopped
Pinch of sugar
Salt and freshly ground black pepper
5 eggs, lightly beaten and seasoned

Choose a large, heavy, frying pan. Heat the olive oil and sauté the onion until it glistens; add the peppers and sauté together for 2-3 minutes. Mix in the tomatoes, herbs, unless using fresh basil which should be added towards the end, sugar and seasoning. Cook uncovered for 15 minutes, stirring occasionally until the sauce has thickened. Pour the eggs over, and add the basil if using fresh. Cook 4-6 minutes, stirring gently with a wooden spatula as for scrambled eggs, until the dish has a creamy, fluid consistency. It is best to take the frying pan to the table and serve immediately with fresh bread and olives.

Chakchouka

Chakchouka has infinite variations, as it may also contain aubergines as in the recipe below, courgettes or almost any other vegetables.

A simple *chakchouka* can be made as for *pipérade* by adding 2 cloves of garlic along with the onions, and once the vegetables have been fried and the tomato sauce reduced to the desired consistency, you should make four small wells in the tomato sauce and drop an egg whole into each one. Season the eggs and cook gently until set.

An Aubergine Chakchouka

This is one of the most interesting, unusual and delicious combinations.

> 6 tablespoons olive oil
> 2 cloves garlic, finely chopped
> 1 green or red pepper, cored, de-seeded and sliced
> 450g (1lb) aubergines, peeled and cubed
> ½ teaspoon ground cummin
> Pinch of cayenne pepper
> 340g (12oz) tomatoes, peeled and chopped
> 2 tablespoons parsley, chopped
> Salt
> 5 eggs, lightly beaten with a little salt

In a large frying pan, heat the olive oil and fry the garlic until aromatic. Add the peppers and aubergine and fry together, turning them until light golden in colour. Add the cummin and cayenne pepper towards the end. Mix in the tomatoes, parsley and salt, and cook gently for 15 minutes. Pour the eggs into the frying pan, stir gently as for scrambled eggs and cook for a further 5 minutes, until set.

VARIATION

This is the Greek version. Omit the onion and the peppers, cook the tomatoes to a pulp in the oil, then add the beaten eggs, and cook gently until the mixture has a scrambled consistency as for *pipérade*.

Menemen
Eggs with Tomatoes and Peppers

TURKEY

An enticing first course or a summery lunch. It is named after the coastal town of Menemeni in western Turkey, where perhaps it originated. It is extremely easy to assemble and make. Choose ripe, sugary tomatoes for the best results.

> 675g (1½lb) tomatoes, peeled and chopped
> 5 tablespoons olive oil
> 1 teaspoon dried marjoram
> Salt and freshly ground black pepper
> ½ teaspoon sugar
> 2 sweet green peppers, cored, de-seeded and chopped
> 55g (2oz) *feta* cheese in small pieces (substitute with Caerphilly)
> 6 eggs, lightly beaten

Pour boiling water over the tomatoes, leave for 10–15 seconds, rinse under cold water and skin them.

In a large frying pan, heat the olive oil and cook the chopped tomatoes with the herbs and seasoning for 15 minutes, stirring occasionally until most of their moisture has evaporated, and a rich sauce is formed. The cooking time will vary according to the ripeness of the tomatoes.

151

Add the sugar and peppers and cook for a further 2–3 minutes. Stir in the cheese, mix well and pour the eggs over. Mix lightly with a fork or wooden spatula as for scrambled eggs. Cook for 4–6 minutes, until the eggs solidify to your taste, and serve.

Tortina Di Carciofi
Omelette with Fresh Globe Artichokes

ITALY

A light and delicate dish, enjoyed at its best when made with young and small artichokes at the dawn of their life. These small artichokes, peeled, sliced and thrown into the frying pan for a few minutes, constitute a delectable imbalance with their youthful and aromatic rawness against the soft and mellow consistency of the eggs. The other ingredient indispensable to the Mediterranean flavour of the dish is, of course, the 'green liquid gold' of the region, the olive oil.

It is known under a variety of different names with slight variations, but it is always delectable. *Frittata di carciofi* or *carciofi in teglia alla Fiorentina* in Italy, *omelette aux artichauts* in France, the Greek *anginares omeletta*, or the Turkish *enginarli yumurta*, are all basically referring to the same dish.

I was thrilled to be served it recently, cooked almost to perfection, in *La Sostanza* – a tiny, white-tiled, workers'

152

trattoria, with long, sturdy communal tables, in the cobbled back streets of the unfashionable part of Florence.

It makes a perfect light lunch, or a first course for dinner.

Serves 2—3

6—8 tablespoons olive oil
2 artichokes
Salt and freshly ground black pepper
5 eggs
1 spring onion, chopped finely (optional)
1 tablespoon fresh dill, chervil *or* parsley, chopped finely
45g (1½oz) freshly grated Parmesan cheese (optional)

In a frying pan, gently heat the olive oil. Prepare each artichoke as described on page 105, wash it, dry it and slice first in half and then each half into 4–5 thin slices. Put these in the frying pan and, when they have all been added, turn up the heat to medium and sauté, turning and coating them in the olive oil, for 5 minutes. Add the seasoning, turn down the heat, cover and cook slowly, turning them occasionally, for a further 8–10 minutes or until soft.

Break the eggs into a large bowl and beat lightly. Add the remaining ingredients and pour over the artichokes. Rotate the frying pan so that the eggs spread evenly. Allow to cook slowly for 3–4 minutes, until it looks set but is still a little runny and soft. Serve immediately.

A Courgette Omelette
GREECE/FRANCE/TURKEY

A refreshingly unusual combination which should be served accompanied by a green salad, comprising different lettuce leaves, watercress, rocket leaves, endives, thin slivers of fennel etc.

340g (12oz) young and firm courgettes (about
   3—4), trimmed, washed and scraped lightly
5 tablespoons olive oil
2 spring onions, skinned, washed and sliced thinly
Salt and freshly ground black pepper
30g (1oz) butter
3 sprigs fresh basil, washed, dried and torn by hand
   or 2 tablespoons chopped fresh dill
4 eggs, beaten lightly with some seasoning

Dry the courgettes and grate them on the thick side of a grater, or put them through a food processor. (Do not be alarmed by the mound of courgette as it shrinks greatly once cooked.)

In a large non-stick frying pan, heat the olive or vegetable oil and sauté the spring onions lightly. Add the grated courgettes and fry rather briskly, turning and tossing them, for about 6–7 minutes. Add the seasoning and the butter, mix and spread the courgettes evenly in the pan.

Mix the chopped herbs into the beaten eggs, and pour evenly on the courgettes. Cook slowly for 3–4 minutes in order to avoid browning the bottom of the omelette. Then, loosen the edges with a wooden spatula and invert the omelette onto a large plate; slip it back into the frying pan and cook it for a further 2–3 minutes so that it retains its soft consistency. Serve immediately.

Tortilla Española
Spanish Omelette

SPAIN

The traditional Spanish omelette, regardless of how we serve omelettes here, is a full meal in itself. It resembles a thick 2.5cm (1in) round cake, but ideally with a soft centre. It

is excellent for picnics, particularly when inserted into a
bocadillo (an elongated fresh bun) like a sandwich. Each
Spanish family produces its own esoteric version of it
according to the season and the availability of fresh
vegetables. The following recipe, however, is the most
familiar, often also containing strips of red and green peppers.
It can be served hot or at room temperature.

> **450g (1lb) potatoes, peeled, washed and sliced very
> finely**
> **Salt**
> **150ml (5fl oz) vegetable oil**
> **1 large onion, skinned and sliced finely**
> **6 eggs**
> **4—5 tablespoons olive oil**

Season the potatoes with salt. In a large frying pan, heat
the vegetable oil. Add the potatoes and onions and fry them
over medium heat, for 15 minutes, turning occasionally,
without letting them brown, until they are properly cooked
and soft. Using a slotted spatula, remove from the pan and
drain off most of the excess oil.

Beat the eggs in a bowl with a little salt, add the potato
mixture and mix well. In a smaller, non-stick frying pan,
heat the olive oil, and pour in the egg mixture, rotating the
pan in order to spread it evenly. Cook over medium heat
at first until it starts to solidify, then turn down the heat
and cook slowly. While cooking, with a wooden spatula, shape
the omelette into a round, pressing the edges away from
the sides of the frying pan.

Shake the pan occasionally, making sure the omelette is
not sticking underneath. This step should take 5–6 minutes.
Place a large plate over the pan and, holding it down with
your left hand and the handle of the pan with your right
(if you are right-handed!) quickly invert the omelette onto
it (without burning yourself). Slide it back into the frying
pan, cooked side uppermost and return to the heat. Cook
it for a further 5–6 minutes, shaping it into a neat circle

155

until it solidifies to your taste. Serve with a crisp, green salad, sharply dressed.

Tortilla de Habas y Ajos Tiernos
Fresh Broad Bean Omelette

This is one of the spring versions of the *tortilla española*. It is very fragrant, using the white part of the stems of fresh garlic. Following the same method you could substitute the beans with fresh artichokes, and another version is made with the first small sugary peas and is equally delicious.

Eggah bi ful akhdar is a similar Arab recipe, made in the Middle East. These Arab *eggah* dishes are mostly baked at gas no. 4 (350°F/180°C) for about 20 minutes until quite firm and lightly brown on top. They, in their turn, are very similar to the French *tian* dishes, and the Greek *sfougato*, all variations on the same theme and all most probably originated or were inspired by the Arab dish. This omelette, like the previous one, can be served hot or at room temperature.

> **675g (1½lb) fresh broad beans with shells**
> **Stems of 3—4 fresh garlics, *or* 2 cloves of garlic**
> **5 tablespoons olive oil**
> **6 eggs**
> **Salt**

Shell the beans, drop them in a saucepan of lightly salted, boiling water, bring back to the boil and cook for 10-15 minutes until soft; drain and reserve. If using fresh garlic, chop the white part of the stems finely. In a non-stick frying pan, heat the olive oil and sauté the garlic until aromatic; add the drained beans and stir for 2 minutes. Remove from the pan with a slotted spatula. Beat the eggs and salt in a bowl, add the beans and garlic and mix well. Pour this into the frying pan and cook as described for *tortilla española* (page 154). Add a little oil if necessary.

Sfougato me Lahanika
Summer Vegetable Pie

GREECE

This is an excellent way of cooking vegetables, a cross between an omelette and a pie, and any combination of vegetables can be treated in the same way. It very much resembles the Arab *eggah*, the French *tian* and, in certain ways, the Spanish omelette – *tortilla española*.

> 675g (1½lb) aubergines, trimmed and cut into
>   thick circles
> 150ml (5fl oz) sunflower oil
> 1 large onion, skinned and sliced finely
> 450g (1lb) courgettes, trimmed, washed and
>   thickly cubed
> 2—3 medium tomatoes, peeled and chopped
> Salt and freshly ground black pepper
> 6 eggs
> 5 tablespoons milk
> 85g (3oz) grated Parmesan cheese, Gruyère, *or*
>   Cheddar cheese
> 2 tablespoons chopped parsley
> 85g (3oz) fresh breadcrumbs

Immerse the aubergines in salted water for 30 minutes, as described on page 112. Dry them and cube them.

Use 2 tablespoons of the sunflower oil to oil a medium sized oven dish, 26 x 26cm/(10 x 10in) or smaller.

In a saucepan, heat the remaining sunflower oil and sauté the onion. Add the courgettes and aubergines and fry over high heat for 3–4 minutes, until they glisten; add the tomatoes, salt and pepper, cover and cook for 15–20 minutes, stirring occasionally, without adding any water. Let it cool.

Beat the eggs with the milk, add half the cheese, and mix together.

Add the parsley, breadcrumbs and the egg mixture to the vegetables, mix and pour evenly into the oven dish. Sprinkle the remaining cheese on top and cook in a preheated oven, gas no. 4 (350°F/180°C), for 30 minutes, until firm and lightly golden on top. Serve immediately or at room temperature.

PULSES AND GRAINS

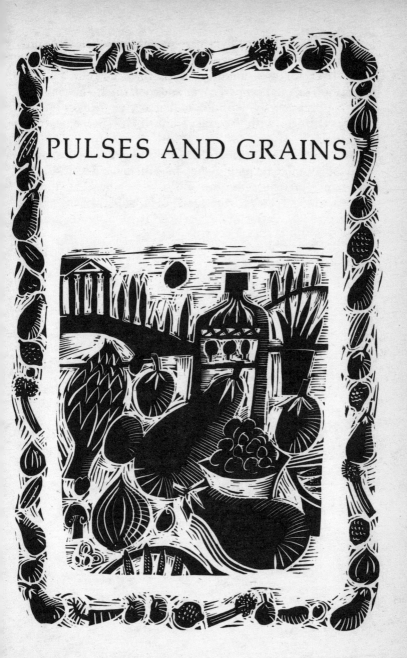

On Pulses

From Plato's Republic – during a conversation defining the various occupations needed in the ideal city, the Symposiasts tackle the need for hired labourers thus:

'Then are there not other agents also who have no mental gifts to make them at all worthy to share in the community, but have bodily strength sufficient for hard labour? They sell the use of their strength, and the price they get for it being called hire, they are known, I fancy, as hired labourers?'

'Certainly.'

'Then these hired labourers, too, serve to complete our city?'

... Here, Glaukon interrupted and said: 'Apparently you give your men dry bread to feast on.'

'You are right,' I said, 'I forgot that they would have a relish with it. They will have salt and olives and cheese, and onions and casseroles made with vegetables such as one gets in the country. And I expect we must allow them a dessert of figs and chickpeas and beans, and they will roast myrtle berries and acorns at the fire and drink their wine in moderation. Leading so peaceful and healthy a life they will naturally attain to a good old age and at death leave their children to live as they have done.'

There are two points clearly illustrated by this extract; first, we can see what was regarded in ancient Greece as a healthy diet – not very different from that of today, namely vegetables, raw and cooked, pulses rich in fibre, fruit and bread. The *ideal* diet for the *Ideal City!*

Second, it stresses the importance of pulses, of beans and chickpeas, as an absolute necessity for a balanced, happy life. Indeed pulses have been popular round the Mediterranean, and particularly its eastern shores, since the sixth and seventh century BC. In Palestine, archaeological finds show that chickpeas were part of the diet as early as the fourth century BC; peas, beans and lentils were cultivated in Assyria and are included in the lists of vegetables of the garden of King Merodach-Baladan of Babylon in the eighth century BC.

Remains of pulses were found in Egyptian tombs, but it seems that these were not popular in Egypt and according to Herodotus, among other comments regarding the diet of the Egyptians, they 'never sow beans and even if any happen to grow wild they will not eat them, either raw or boiled.' (P. Brothwell, *Food in Antiquity.*)

Large earthenware jars (*pythoi*), dating from neolithic times, with the remains of chickpeas, broad beans and lentils have been found in Crete. There are also various references to pulses from the ancient Greek playwrights, some scornful and ironic, but, nevertheless, painting quite a descriptive image of the multi-faceted uses of pulses and their popularity not only as food, but for casting votes and as part of ritual offerings to the gods.

Indeed, pulses were so popular that in ancient Greece they were also street-food or, in present-day terminology, 'fast food', in the same way that hot, spicy *tamia – falafel*, made out of broad beans or chickpeas, is sold nowadays on almost every street corner in the Lebanon, Israel and Egypt.

In Athens, a kind of porridge called *etnos* was made with either broad beans (which was also the most popular), peas, or lentils. This was not only served at home but was also made in the streets by special cooks who sold it from their bubbling cauldrons to passers-by. Various references to *etnos* are made by Aristophanes but, unfortunately, he does not indicate the full method of preparation; Apicius, however, later on, does and, according to him, once the pulses were boiled and pulped they were mixed with olive oil and ingredients such as honey, wine, vinegar or egg yolks and cooked a little longer. *Etnos* was considered quite indigestible but extremely nourishing. Appropriately then, it was recorded as Hercules' favourite food and Aristophanes jokes about him by calling him greedy for *etnos* in *The Frogs*.

Chickpeas, according to Greek mythology, were found by Poseidon, wrathful God of the Sea, and they are mentioned both by Homer and the Lesbian poetess Sappho.

In Italy, pulses were also popular and Roman literature is studded with references, even though one has the impression from these references that pulses were considered lowly food for the proletariat. Horace, in his *Economical Diet*, aptly describes 'onions, pulses and pancakes'. And Pliny, who was quite disparaging of the affluent gastronomic extravagances of his contemporaries, highly recommended pulses. According to *Apicius de Re Quoquinaria* in 1498, which is the work of an editor much later than Apicius, who was a gourmet during the reign of Tiberius, pulses were cooked in various ways: lentils, for instance, were cooked with mussels, chestnuts or with salted anchovies; and there is even nowadays a Catalonian dish, *lentejas y anchoas*, which is clearly derived from the ancient dish that it closely resembles.

Broad beans were extremely popular in ancient Greece, particularly among the lower classes. They were cooked either fresh or dried and also offered raw as appetizers when fresh, according to Athenaeos, the second-century AD writer. They were even cooked in a special pot which was called a *seison*. Particularly favoured were those from the Aegean island of Limnos, as Aristophanes appropriately praises them in the *Limniai: 'Limnos kyamous trefousa takerous kai kalous.'* (Limnos produces beans that are tasty and tender.)

Dioskoridis, the first-century AD writer from Anazarba in Cilicia, in his *Greek Herbal*, refers in detail to their medicinal qualities as well as their pitfalls, as he does with the rest of the pulses:

> The Greek bean is windey, flatulent, hard of digestion
> causing troublesomme dreames; yet good for the
> Cough, and breeding flesh being in ye midst of hott
> and cold. Being sod [boiled] with Oxymel, and eaten
> with the Shucks [skins], it stays dysenteries and the
> fluxes of the Coeliaci [bowel], and being eaten it is
> good against vomiting. But it is made lesse flatulent,
> if the first water in which it was sod be cast away.

This last remark is extraordinary, for even today most pulses
in Greece, as indeed in other countries too, are briefly
brought to the boil and drained, in order to make them more
digestible and less flatulent, as Dioskoridis suggested all that
time ago. This much for continuity!

Beans had even had a god assigned to them – Apollo –
and there was a special celebration in his honour in Attica,
called *Pyanepsia*. *Pyanepsia* was the equivalent of the Harvest
Festival in Britain, celebrating the harvesting of the various
crops but not including wheat, which had another special
feast called *Thalysia*. On the day of the *Pyanepsia*, boiled broad
beans were offered to the god. In addition, it was imperative
for each family to boil together a selection of pulses, which
was called *panspermia* (*pan* = everything, *sperma* = seed), to be
eaten by all members of the family and also offered to the
dead. Broad bean plants were considered inauspicious and
carried connotations of death; perhaps this was the reason
that broad beans were offered to the dead as well as to the
deities of the Underworld, particularly the dreaded Hades.

That beans and lentils were so popular in antiquity is also
illustrated by the fact that there was a whole philosophical
school, the Pythagorians, that objected to them and its
members were not allowed to eat them. One of the strongest
theories for their rejection was along the following lines:
beans make wind and wind is a sign of life (like breath for
instance); life is caused by souls, therefore beans are people.
And the moral of this? Eating beans is a kind of cannibalism.

Another simpler explanation emerges from the following
extract from Cicero's *De Divinatione*, based on a conversation

from Plato's *Symposium*. In comparing Plato's thinking with the ideas of Epicurus, the argument proceeds thus: 'Will you then, put this man [Epicurus] before Plato or Socrates, who though they gave no reason, would yet prevail over these petty philosophers by the mere weight of their name? Now Plato's advice to us is to set out for the land of dreams with bodies so prepared that no error or confusion may assail the soul. For this reason, it is thought, the Pythagorians were forbidden to indulge in beans; for that food produces great flatulence and induces a condition at war with a soul in search of truth.'

There we have it all! Throughout the ages, pulses have been the stuff on which life is sustained; and nowadays with much improved varieties and ways to counteract their flatulence-producing tendencies, who knows, even Plato might have been converted. As far as I am concerned, when I think of a bubbling pot of bean soup or of *saucisson aux flageolets*, I am with Epicurus all the way!

Garbanzos a la Vinagreta
Chickpeas with Vinaigrette Sauce

A popular dish, which is tasty and easy. It can be served as a main course or as part of a large *tapas* table.

> 225g (8oz) chickpeas, picked clean and soaked
>   overnight
> 1 medium onion, skinned and sliced
> 1 ham bone *or* 2 slices lean bacon, chopped
> 2 bay leaves
> Salt

VINAIGRETTE

- 6 tablespoons olive oil
- 2 tablespoons wine vinegar
- 2 cloves garlic, peeled and crushed
- 1 hard-boiled egg, shelled
- 1 tablespoon capers, rinsed and drained
- 3 tablespoons mixed fresh green herbs such as parsley, chervil, dill etc.
- 2 medium tomatoes, peeled, de-seeded and diced

Rinse and drain the chickpeas. Place them in a large saucepan with the onion, ham bone or bacon and bay leaves, cover with plenty of cold water, bring to the boil and skim until clear. Add salt, cover and simmer until the chickpeas are tender, approximately 1 hour according to their age. Drain them and, if you wish, reserve their broth for a vegetable soup.

Meanwhile, make the vinaigrette. In a bowl, lightly beat the olive oil, vinegar and garlic. Mash the hard-boiled egg yolk and mix in. Chop the egg white and add with the remaining ingredients, mixing well. Pour this over the hot chickpeas and stir until well coated.

Garbanzos y Judias con Espinacas

Chickpeas and Beans with Spinach Casserole

SPAIN

An unusual combination, reminiscent perhaps of Arab cuisine, where pulses and greens are often combined. However, in medieval Arab dishes the cooking medium was often fat from a sheep's tail, and in traditional Spanish cuisine the dish called for *manteca de cerdo* – a solid piece of pig's fat – as in a number of Spanish and French peasant dishes. Other

kinds of greens are also often used in Spain, such as beet
– *acelgas* – or Swiss chard. One could also use spring greens.

Serves 6

225g (8oz) chickpeas, picked clean and soaked
  overnight
5 tablespoons olive oil *or* good quality vegetable
  oil
1 large onion, skinned and chopped
1 whole head garlic, peeled and chopped
110g (4oz) *chorizo or* streaky bacon, chopped
1 bay leaf
Salt
4—5 black peppercorns
225g (8oz) cannellini *or* haricot beans, cleaned and
  soaked overnight
450g (1lb) spinach *or* beetroot tops, trimmed

Wash and drain the chickpeas. Place them in a large saucepan,
cover them with cold water by about 5cm (2in) above their
surface, bring to the boil and skim. Add the olive or vegetable
oil, the onion, garlic and *chorizo* or chopped bacon, bay leaf
and seasoning. Bring back to the boil, cover and simmer for
about 1 hour, until tender.

Place the cannellini or haricot beans in a saucepan, cover
them with cold water, bring to the boil, cover and simmer
for about 40 minutes until tender. Drain.

Wash the spinach or beetroot tops meticulously until no
trace of grit remains, then shred them. Blanch briefly in
a large saucepan of boiling, salted water and drain.

Add the beans and spinach or beetroot tops to the
chickpeas, adjust the seasoning, cover and simmer for a
further 10 minutes, to blend the flavours.

Garbanzos a la Catalana

Catalonian Chickpea Casserole

This is one of the better known and oldest Spanish dishes. It is also one of the most delicious. *Butifarra* is a spiced, cummin-scented pork sausage.

> 450g (1lb) chickpeas, picked clean and soaked overnight
> 5 tablespoons good quality vegetable oil
> 2 onions, skinned and chopped
> 45g (1½oz) pine kernels
> 340g (12oz) tomatoes, peeled, de-seeded and chopped
> 140g (5oz) *butifarra*, thinly sliced *or* herby sausages
> Salt and freshly ground black pepper
> 2 hard-boiled eggs, shelled and chopped

Wash and drain the chickpeas. Place them in a large saucepan with plenty of water; bring to the boil and skim, then cover and simmer for 20 minutes. Drain, reserving the liquid.

In a large frying pan, heat the vegetable oil and brown the onions lightly. Add the pine kernels and sauté for a further 1–2 minutes, then mix in the tomatoes and stir until thickened. Lastly, add the *butifarra* or sausages and fry for a few minutes.

Put the chickpeas in an oven-proof casserole – preferably earthenware – pour in the onion mixture, seasoning and 300ml (10fl oz) of the chickpea liquid. Stir well, cover and cook in a preheated oven, gas no. 3 (325°F/160°C), for 1½ hours. Stir occasionally and add a little more liquid if needed, but there should be a thick sauce. Sprinkle the chopped, hard-boiled eggs on top and serve.

Ful Medames
Small Egyptian Brown Beans

EGYPT

Ancient like the Pharoahs or not, this is undoubtedly the national dish of Egypt. The small, round, dark brown beans – a kind of broad bean but of a round shape – have an earthy, basic but unique taste that has nourished generations of Egyptians of all classes. It is sold in the streets, often tucked neatly into *pitta* bread with rings of raw onions and tomatoes.

> 450g (1lb) *full medames*, picked and clean and
>   soaked overnight
> Salt and freshly ground black pepper
> 2—3 cloves garlic, peeled and crushed
>
> **GARNISHES**
>
> Small bowl of finely chopped parsley
> 2 lemons, quartered
> Olive oil
> 4 hard-boiled eggs, shelled

Rinse the beans, cover well with cold water and bring to the boil; cover and simmer gently for about 1½ hours, until the beans are tender but not falling apart. Drain them, put in a bowl with a little of the cooking liquid and mix with the seasoning and garlic. Allow people to serve themselves in individual bowls, offering them the indispensable garnishes and a boiled egg each. A generous quantity of olive oil and lemon is vital to the taste of the dish. A favourite and homely way to eat *ful medames* is to lightly mash the egg and the beans together with a fork, once all the ingredients have been added, in order to tame the almost wild taste of the beans.

Flageolets aux Saucissons

Flageolets Beans with Sausages

Perhaps, one might think, a humble and simple dish; but its taste is enriched with many flavours. Particularly if one strikes upon a tasty batch of beans.

> 340g (12oz) flageolet beans, picked clean and
>   soaked overnight
> 5 tablespoons vegetable oil
> 1 large onion, skinned and sliced finely
> 2 cloves garlic, peeled and chopped
> 2 tablespoons tomato purée
> 1 litre (1¾ pints) water
> 1 tablespoon thyme
> Salt and freshly ground black pepper
> 450g (1lb) Toulouse sausages *or* similar herby-
>   flavoured sausages

Rinse and drain the beans. In a large saucepan, heat the vegetable oil and fry the onion and garlic until light golden in colour. Mix in the beans and stir until they are well coated in the oil. Add all the remaining ingredients, except the sausages, cover and cook for 1 hour, stirring occasionally.

Meanwhile, slice the sausages into 8cm (3in) pieces and fry briefly in a dry frying pan for 3–4 minutes only, in order to get rid of their excess fat. Remove the sausages with a slotted spoon and drain off their oil before adding them to the casserole of beans. Mix well, cover and cook gently for a further 15 minutes.

Kitchri or Kushuri

Lentils with Rice

Kitchri or *kushuri* is everyday fast food in the crowded, colourful streets of Cairo, as popular as *tamia* or perhaps even more so. It consists of brown lentils cooked with rice, and sometimes boiled macaroni is added to make the dish more substantial. A garnish of fried onions and a tomato and chilli sauce give it its flavour.

According to my friend Sami Zubaida, 'It is dispensed from mobile stalls or from hole-in-the-wall *kushuri* restaurants or snack bars. *Kushuri*, while not a gastronomic event, is very cheap and filling fast food, enjoyed by working people for lunch or on their way to and from work.'

Claudia Roden in her *Middle Eastern Food* mentions also a similar dish of lentils and rice of medieval origin, described by al-Baghdadi as food for the poor, under the name of *mujadarra*.

A very similar recipe called *moutzendra* is popular in Cyprus and this is undoubtedly of Arab origin. Strangely enough, a rather simplified version is popular in a number of Greek Aegean islands, while virtually unknown on the Greek mainland. Clearly this is a dish that followed history in the Aegean, and one can mark its route by the conquests, during the eighth century, of the strong Arab fleets and Saracen pirates of the time.

When spiced appropriately, *kushuri*, *mujadarra*, *moutzendra*, or whatever other name it may bear, is an appetizing dish with a unique earthiness about it.

The following recipe is Sami Zubaida's, as he introduced us to the dish and because of his passion for it. Although the recipe calls for butter, this can be substituted with olive oil or groundnut oil, particularly if the dish is to be cooked in advance or served at room temperature.

225g (8oz) long-grain rice (Basmati for best
   results), washed and drained
225g (8oz) brown or Egyptian lentils (even better
   are the Indian waxy *tur dal*)
110g (4oz) butter *or* 150ml (5fl oz) olive oil
4—6 cloves garlic, peeled and chopped
1—2 tablespoons ground cummin
1 tablespoon tomato purée
Salt and freshly ground black pepper

FOR OPTIONAL GARNISH

1 medium onion, skinned and sliced in rings
110g (4oz) Haloumi cheese *or* a hard Gruyère
   cheese, sliced
2 tomatoes, sliced

If Basmati rice is used it should be washed, soaked in cold
water for 30 minutes then drained. Pick the lentils clean,
wash them, place them in a large saucepan and cover with
cold water. Bring to the boil, cover and simmer for 10–15
minutes, until almost cooked. Drain.

In a saucepan, melt half the butter or olive oil and sauté
the garlic gently and briefly. Add the cummin and fry for
a few more seconds, then mix in the drained rice and lentils,
so that the grains are coated with the butter and spices.
Add the tomato purée and mix well. Pour in water to cover
by about 1cm (½in) and season with salt and pepper to taste.
Bring to the boil on a high flame, then reduce the flame
to medium and allow the liquid to be absorbed. When only
a few bubbles remain on the surface, reduce the heat to
a minimum, cover tightly and allow to steam for about 15
minutes.

To make the garnish, in a frying pan, fry the onion rings
in the remaining butter or oil until lightly browned, and
then spread them on top of the rice. Fry the slices of cheese
on both sides until lightly browned. Remove and reserve.

Finally, fry the tomatoes until soft, then add with the cheese to the onion rings.

Serve *kitchri* on a platter with the garnish spread all over the top, and accompanied by bowls of yoghurt and/or a yoghurt drink such as the Turkish *ayran*, on page 203.

Lentejas con Morcilla
Lentil Casserole

SPAIN

Morcilla resembles *butifarra* (see page 103) in that it is also made with pork and its blood, but it is thinner in appearance and not as spicy but it has a strong, smoked flavour. One could use black pudding but, because it lacks the spicing, I prefer to use some spicy sausages or even some streaky bacon, just to add some richness to the final flavour of the dish.

225g (8oz) brown lentils
1 bay leaf
6 tablespoons olive oil
3 cloves garlic, peeled but left whole
1 large onion, skinned and chopped finely
1 teaspoon plain flour
1 teaspoon *pimentón* (see page 104) *or* paprika
110g (4oz) *morcilla or* spicy sausages *or* streaky
    bacon, chopped
Salt and freshly ground black pepper
2 crustless slices of bread, fried in vegetable oil and
    drained

Pick the lentils clean and wash them. Place them in a large saucepan with the bay leaf and cover with cold water. Bring to the boil, cover and simmer for 25 minutes. Drain, reserving some of the liquid. In a large frying pan, heat the olive oil

173

and fry the garlic until pale golden in colour and remove. Brown the onion lightly in the same oil, add the flour and *pimentón*, and the sausage or bacon and sauté for 2 minutes. Mix in the lentils and seasoning and stir together for a few more minutes.

Meanwhile, place the fried bread and garlic with 3 tablespoons of the lentil liquid in a food processor or blender and blend briefly. Mix this into the lentils, add a teacup of the lentil liquid and simmer for a further 10 minutes, until the flavours have blended.

GRAINS

Burani
A Princely Pilaff
TURKEY/GREECE/YUGOSLAVIA

If you have read the introduction to aubergines (page 110), you will know the glittering course of events that led to *burani* – originally a family of aubergine dishes cooked for Buran's wedding in ninth-century Baghdad, or perhaps cooked by the bride herself at some later occasion. How could this lead to the present day *burani* which bears no relation to aubergines? Such are the mysteries of culinary evolution! Although in Turkey this is a popular dish, in Greece it is only Greek refugees from Asia Minor and Istanbul who commonly cook it and call it by this name. To most other Greeks *burani* will probably be just a puzzling word. This indicates that the original dish was elaborated on and altered by the addition of grain in Turkey. Weren't the Ottomans great lovers of rice and aren't Turkish pilaffs monumental and referred to by all sorts of literature, throughout the ages? Even Paradise has been parodied as a series of pilaff-mountains in Turkish folklore. The most delicious *burani* I have tasted was cooked by our next-door neighbours in Athens, a family of refugees from Smyrna after the catastrophic war of 1922. The beauty of this dish relies undoubtedly on the large amount of sweet summer tomatoes, garlic and olive oil.

> 90ml (3fl oz) olive oil
> 3—4 cloves garlic, peeled and chopped finely
> 450g (1lb) ripe tomatoes, peeled and chopped
> 425ml (15fl oz) water
> Large pinch of allspice
> Pinch of cinnamon
> ¼ teaspoon sugar
> Salt and freshly ground black pepper
> 225g (8oz) long-grain rice
> 2 tablespoons finely chopped parsley

In a large saucepan, heat the olive oil and sauté the garlic briefly without browning it. Add all the remaining ingredients, except the rice and parsley, bring to the boil, cover and simmer for 5 minutes. Then mix in the rice and parsley. Stir well, cover and cook gently until the water has been absorbed, approximately 15-20 minutes. The dish should be quite moist at the end, but on no account should the rice be overcooked. Serve with Egyptian *tamia* (page 53), or some fried squid.

Bulguri Pilafi
Cracked Wheat and Vermicelli

CYPRUS

This surprisingly tasty dish, with its earthy pleasing aroma, is quickly assembled from a combination of humble ingredients. It can be served as a main meal, accompanied by any of the dishes in the Appetizers section and with bowls of plain, preferably sheep's, yoghurt on the table.

The cracked wheat (*burghul*) should be picked clean of little stones etc. first.

> 120ml (4fl oz) olive oil *or* groundnut oil
> 1 large onion, skinned and sliced finely
> 45g (1½oz) vermicelli
> 225g (8oz) cracked wheat (*burghul*), picked clean, washed and drained
> 300ml (10fl oz) chicken stock
> Salt and freshly ground black pepper

In a saucepan, heat the olive or groundnut oil and lightly brown the onion; add the vermicelli, breaking it with your hands. Sauté for 3–4 minutes until the mixture looks pale golden in colour. Add the cracked wheat to the saucepan. Pour in the chicken stock, with seasoning to taste, and mix well. Bring to the boil, cover and simmer very gently for about 6 minutes, until all the liquid has evaporated. Remove the lid and cover the top of the saucepan with a clean tea towel. Place the lid tightly on top and let it stand for 10 minutes before serving. (You will be surprised at the delicious smell when you uncover the saucepan.) Covered like this, it will keep hot and fresh for about 1 hour. Fluff the grains a little with a fork before serving.

If there is some left, it will still be grainy and equally delicious if reheated with 3–4 tablespoons of water the next day.

Riso Con Fagioli Alla Fiorentina

Rice with Cannellini Beans

ITALY

An interesting dish, sturdy but extremely tasty. The *pancetta*, which adds flavour, can be replaced by streaky bacon. The hot pepper – the *peperoncino* – can be replaced by a large pinch of cayenne pepper. White kidney or cannellini beans, popular in Florentine cooking, are used, but one can experiment with other types of beans. *Borlotti* beans, for instance, with their scarlet and creamy stripes, make an enticing alternative.

In Italy, in the early summer, it is also made with shelled fresh cannellini beans, when it resembles a spring dish of shelled fresh broad beans with rice, which can be found not only in Italy but also in Greece and Turkey.

> **225g (8oz) cannellini beans, picked clean and soaked overnight**
> **60ml (2fl oz) olive oil**
> **85g (3oz) *pancetta or* streaky bacon, diced**
> **1 medium onion, skinned and chopped finely**
> **3 cloves garlic, peeled and chopped finely**
> **1 green or red chilli, de-seeded and chopped *or* large pinch cayenne pepper**
> **396g (14oz) can of tomatoes, chopped *or* 450g (1lb) fresh tomatoes, peeled and chopped**
> **Salt**
> **110g (4oz) long-grain rice *or* Patna rice, washed and drained**
> **2—3 tablespoons chopped parsley**
> **2—3 sprigs fresh basil *or* ½ teaspoon dried basil**

Wash and drain the beans. Place in a large saucepan, cover well with fresh water, bring to the boil and boil for 5 minutes; drain. Heat the olive oil in the saucepan and fry the diced *pancetta* or bacon for two minutes. Add the onion, garlic and chilli and sauté until lightly coloured.

Mix in the beans, tomatoes and salt, and enough cold water to cover them by about 5cm (2in). Bring to the boil, cover and cook until the beans are softer but preferably not fully cooked; this would take about 5 minutes in a pressure cooker, otherwise it may take about 45 minutes.

Add the drained rice, parsley and dried basil, if using. Cover and simmer for a further 15 minutes, until the rice is cooked. Sprinkle with fresh basil, if using, and serve hot.

SALADS

Mediterranean Markets

When visiting foreign lands, I find that a trip to a local market puts the country and its culture into a clearer perspective. Immerse yourself in the soft colours of the luscious fruit and vegetables, listen to the cries of the vendors, blending with the noise of the city beyond the often invisible but magical walls of the market, and you will emerge immensely more knowledgeable.

Walk up the narrow cobbled streets of Pera in Istanbul and enter the Beyoglou market and you will discover what the salad you will eat at lunchtime looks like. There are the bunches of dark green *roka* – rocket, with its sharp bitter taste, coupled with the crisp lettuces in the basket beneath, and crowned by the scarlet beauty of the minute radishes, a fiery note among the autumnal greenery; then there is the sparkling green plumage of the flat-leaved parsley, and the young, fleshy purslane. All these are set against a background of fierce, vibrant green chillies. (How hot these are you will also discover at lunchtime – I did, anyway!)

A little further along, there are tubs of fresh cheeses – the crumbly, savoury *beyaz peynir*, spilling out of dark goat skins, and the *peynir tulum* – with their sharp enticing flavours and aromas. It is *beyaz peynir* which, coupled with the sweetest of melons in Turkey, plays an important role among the *mezze*.

Fresh wet walnuts, too, are to be found and beautifully arranged baskets of purple figs, grapes, and more grapes, of various hues and sizes.

If the variety and excitement is a little overwhelming, walk across the road to the old and genteel establishment of the

181

Konak for some hot tea, and sample a few of those delights that crumble in the mouth, sweeter than the sweetest of dreams. Indulge yourself in the burnt, candied top of a creamy *kazan dibi*, the unusual Turkish pudding made with shredded chicken breasts, or the honey-moist *seker pare*. If you are lucky on the day, you may even have a bowl of rose-scented, gelatinous *asure* – Noah's pudding – said to contain forty different ingredients, from wheat to dried fruit and pulses.

Or cross the elevated pavement of the tree-lined *Ramblas* in Barcelona on a bright March morning, passing the flower and bird sellers, and enter the dark San José market. Ponder on the size of the first young sweet peas, the pale broad beans, the firm, perfectly petalled artichokes, the innumerable bunches of curly chervil; all accentuated and brought to life by the sparkling, poppy-coloured beauty of the sweet peppers, whose flavour cannot be surpassed.

Deeper into the market, the large, shallow, marble sinks are full of the salted fillets of *bacalao* (cod) soaking for the *esqueixada* that awaits you at lunchtime in the low-ceilinged Gardenia Restaurant, at the opposite end of the market. *Esqueixada*, a favourite Catalan speciality, is a rather robust salad, served as a first course, and consists of a bed of diced tomatoes, peppers, black olives and sweet sharp onion rings with shredded, raw, salted cod on top and the whole dressed with olive oil.

Next, and in prime position, are the displays of the salted and smoked fish, the little silvery *mariquitas*, the *sardinas*, among the sparkling flakes of salt and, last on the line, the half-moon shaped little pies filled with salted cod, ready to fry or bake, the *empanadillas de brandada*. All this produce quite obviously important to the Spanish culinary tradition and its fasting patterns.

But for the best salad ingredients you have to visit the spectacular nineteenth-century cast-iron *Mercato Centrale* – the covered market in Florence. There you will find a bewildering assortment of leaves and more leaves. Basket after basket overflowing with the bitter green stalks of *rughetta* – rocket, the bitter, striped purple leaves of different shapes, sizes and hues of *radichio* and *trevisano*, the *crescione* – watercress, the *salvastrella*, the *quercholina* – oak salad, and the mild tasting, bright green blades of the *minutina* or *barba di cappuchino*, whose colour may not resemble the beard of a monk, as its name suggests, but which could well be mistaken for tender grass. These, mixed with curly endive and chicory or a few crisp leaves of iceberg or cos lettuce and dressed with the best Lucca olive oil and fresh lemon, make the most glorious combinations and provide a mosaic of warm colours such as is only displayed in the most precious Anatolian rugs.

Grilled Pepper Salad

ITALY/SPAIN

In Italy bright peppers of different colours, waxy yellows, explosive reds and sparkling greens, are used for this appetizing dish, which resembles very much the Spanish *escalibada*. It is invaluable and vital for mixed *antipasti*, or on its own as a first course, and is excellent with smoked salmon or a fish starter such as the Greek *taramosalata*. It not only looks good but it also has a sensational taste.

    4 sweet peppers of mixed colour, wiped clean
    7 tablespoons olive oil
    1—2 cloves garlic, peeled and crushed
    Salt and freshly ground black pepper
    ½ teaspoon oregano

Place the peppers under a hot grill and turn them until they become blistered and charred all over. When they are slightly cooled (but still hot otherwise they will be difficult to peel), peel them. Core and de-seed them and slice in long strips.

183

Lay the strips in one layer on a boldly coloured platter. About 15 minutes before they are to be served, mix the olive oil with the remaining ingredients and pour it over the peppers.

Salade Niçoise

Salade Niçoise is more substantial than an ordinary salad and makes a filling first course or a light lunch.

> 340g (12oz) tomatoes, washed, trimmed and quartered
> 1 sweet green pepper, washed, cored, de-seeded and cut in rings
> 1 small onion, skinned and cut in rings
> 8 or more black olives, preferably Niçois
> 5 tablespoons good olive oil
> Salt and freshly ground black pepper
> 2 hard-boiled eggs, shelled and quartered
> 4 anchovy fillets, cut in half
> 6—8 basil leaves, shredded by hand

In a bowl, combine all the ingredients up to and including salt and pepper and toss gently. Empty onto a platter, surround with the quarters of hard-boiled egg, dot with the anchovies and sprinkle the basil over the top.

If you wish to make this more substantial, you can add a boiled and cubed potato and a small handful of boiled young French beans.

Fagioli Con Tonno

Beans with Tuna

ITALY/TUSCANY

One of the best known Tuscan dishes, this is deservedly included in every collection of cold *antipasti*.

> 170g (6oz) cannellini *or* haricot beans, cleaned and
>   soaked overnight
> 1 medium onion (the red variety if possible),
>   skinned and sliced finely
> 6 tablespoons olive oil
> 1 tablespoon wine vinegar
> 1 x 198g (7oz) can of tuna, preferably drained of its
>   oil, and flaked
> 2 tablespoons chopped chervil *or* parsley
> Salt and freshly ground black pepper

Rinse and drain the beans. Place in a large saucepan with plenty of water and bring to the boil. Cover and simmer for about 45 minutes or until tender. Drain and place them in a bowl. Add all the remaining ingredients, toss gently, and serve.

Spicy Potato and Cauliflower Salad
MOROCCO

A spicy dish that can be made using a different selection of vegetables, e.g. cauliflower and carrots, or courgettes and potato. Also raw radishes, white or red, or a kholrabi, peeled and cubed could be added. In most North African dishes, particularly those from Tunisia and Morocco, the use of a spicy mixture called *harissa* is vital for the character of the

185

dish. This is made from dried chillies, ground coriander, ground cummin seeds and garlic. However, small imported tins of *harissa* can be found in ethnic stores. Alternatively you can improvise at home – as long as you are not entertaining the Tunisian ambassador!

½ small cauliflower, cored and broken into florets
450g (1lb) small potatoes, washed and lightly
  scraped
1 teaspoon *harissa* diluted in 2 tablespoons water*
½ teaspoon ground cummin
5 tablespoons olive oil
Juice of ½ lemon and the grated zest
2 tablespoons parsley, chopped finely
1 tablespoon fresh coriander, chopped finely
Lemon quarters, to garnish

*QUICK HARISSA SUBSTITUTE

¼ teaspoon chilli powder
¼ teaspoon ground coriander
¼ teaspoon ground cummin
1 clove garlic, peeled and crushed

Boil the cauliflower in lightly salted boiling water for about 4 minutes, until slightly tender (use it raw if you prefer). Drain and reserve. Boil the potatoes for about 15–20 minutes until tender but not falling apart. (This is always more successful with the potatoes unpeeled.) Drain and, when cooler, skin and cube.

Mix all the remaining ingredients in a bowl and beat lightly with a fork. Add the vegetables and toss them gently in the sauce until well coated. Turn out on a platter and serve with quartered lemons.

Hindiba Salatassi

Endive Salad

Get two or three heads of endive*, remove
the dark green leaves, pick off the others one
by one, and cut the large ones in two; wash
and drain them in a cloth, by shaking it to
and fro violently, and extract all the water;
then put in the salad bowl a small teaspoonful
of salt, one or two pinches of pepper, the
juice of a small lemon, three tablespoonfuls
of olive oil and beat up until it becomes like
cream, then put in the salad, and turn it with
spoon and fork till well mixed, and serve.

A tablespoonful of chopped chervil and one
of chives is a great improvement. Dandelion
may be dressed the same. (Turabi Effendi)

Also known as frisée.

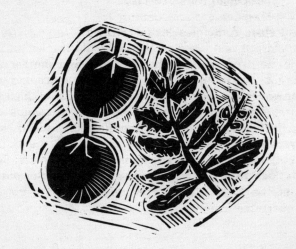

Artichoke and Orange Salad
MOROCCO

As they are so plentiful there, oranges are often used in salads in Morocco and Tunisia. One sees orange, lemon and bitter orange trees planted along streets, in public gardens and in every single back garden of even humble households. Oranges are mixed with olives, or boiled potatoes or carrots in different combinations – in fact whatever the kitchen garden or local market allows on the day.

3 tablespoons olive oil
½ lemon, peeled and quartered
Salt
2 tablespoons lemon juice
4 artichoke hearts, quartered (see page 105)
2 tablespoons sugar
300ml (10fl oz) water
1 large orange, peeled, de-seeded and sliced into
    2.5cm (1in) thick rounds

In a saucepan, combine a little water with the olive oil, ½ lemon and salt and bring to the boil. Add the lemon juice and the prepared artichoke hearts, cover and simmer until tender, about 15 minutes; drain and reserve artichokes only.

Meanwhile, in a saucepan, dissolve the sugar in the 300ml (10fl oz) water, bring to the boil and reduce the liquid until lightly thickened. Quarter the orange slices, add them to the syrup and cook for 2–3 minutes. Add the drained artichokes and mix well. Empty onto a platter and serve chilled. You can dust with a little cayenne pepper or paprika if you prefer.

Chalda Bartogal Wa Jazar

Orange and Carrot Salad

A fragrant salad, adapted from Arto der Haroutunian's book, *North African Cookery.*

> 1 orange, peeled with most of the white pith
>   removed
> 340g (12oz) carrots, peeled and grated
> 1 tablespoon sugar
> 2 tablespoons orange flower water
> Juice of 1 orange
> 30g (1oz) toasted pine kernels

Slice the orange into thin rounds and then into quarters. Remove the pips. Mix with all the remaining ingredients, except the pine kernels, in a bowl, toss and let stand for about 10 minutes at room temperature. Toss again, sprinkle the pine kernels on top and serve.

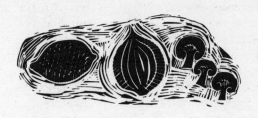

Tomato and Mozzarella Salad

ITALY

Arranged beautifully, this salad looks like a vibrant tapestry. It really belongs more to the family of the *antipasti* – the appetizers – rather than the salads. Try to use fresh basil as it makes an enormous difference to the flavour.

225g (8oz) ripe tomatoes, peeled and sliced in circles
170g (6oz) packet fresh mozzarella cheese
Salt (optional)
6—8 tablespoons olive oil
Some basil leaves, shredded a little by hand

Arrange the tomatoes on a flat dish in overlapping rows, then place extremely thin slices of mozzarella cheese on top of them. Just before serving, sprinkle over a little salt (if using; salt detracts from the taste of sweet ripe tomatoes), then drizzle the oil over, and lastly add the basil.

DESSERTS AND SHERBETS

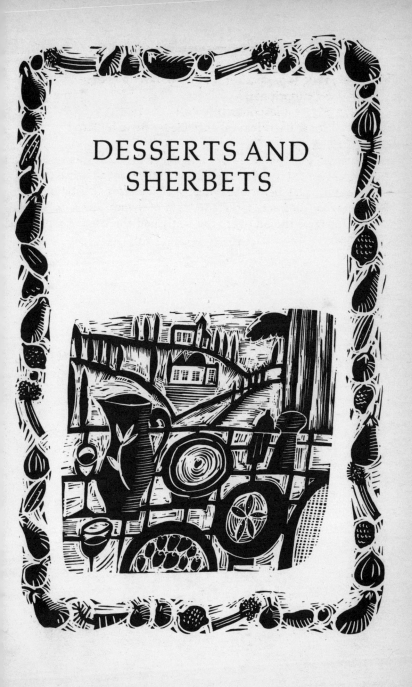

The Opulence of Mediterranean Fruit

The skin of the watermelon is green, smooth and thin. The inside is a purple pulp, studded with broad, flat, black seeds and impregnated with a juice the most cool, delicate and refreshing, that can well be conceived. One would imagine the pulp itself dissolved in the stomach; for you may eat of it until you are filled up to the tongue, without feeling any inconvenience. It is so friendly to the constitution, that, in ardent inflammatory fevers, it is drunk as the best emulsion. At Genoa, Florence, and Rome it is sold in the streets, ready cut in slices; and the porters sweating under their burdens, buy and eat them as they pass. A porter of London quenches his thirst with a draught of strong beer. A porter of Rome or Naples, refreshes himself with a slice of watermelon, or a glass of iced-water.... It is commonly remarked that beer strengthens as well as refreshes, but the porters of Constantinople, who never drink anything stronger than water and eat very little animal food, will lift and carry heavier burdens than any other porters in the known world.
(Tobias Smollett)

Even though the olive tree is the cornerstone of Mediterranean flora, there is also the brilliant world of the fruit trees: glorious, cheap and abundant! A variety of a thousand and one, like the Arabian Nights! Figs, dates, pomegranates, melons, mulberries, apricots, peaches, pears,

193

apples, oranges, lemons, mandarins ... the variety, size, colour and fragrance of Mediterranean fruit are astounding and a pleasure to behold. Mountains of colourful fruit, moist and sugary, surprise you round each corner, on trestle tables, or market stalls, in push-carts and, quite often still, mule- or donkey-drawn carts with vendors advertising, at the tops of their voices, the merits of their loads from neighbourhood to neighbourhood.

Because of its abundance and relatively low cost, particularly at the height of its season, fruit is a major part of Mediterranean diet and life. It does not constitute a luxury prescribed to be eaten ceremoniously at set times of the day. Some juicy peaches or figs may be eaten at breakfast; a slice of aromatic melon or cooling watermelon will be devoured in the course of a summer morning, as by the porters of Rome and Naples in 1766, in the passage above. Italians serve melon or figs with Parma ham as *antipasti*. Sweet melon accompanied by white crumbly cheese – *beyaz peynir* – is always part of the *mezze* in Turkey.

Fruit is also offered to visitors, according to Mediterranean custom – a bowl of scarlet strawberries, or an assorted platter of peeled and sliced seasonal fruit, melons and watermelons mixed with sweet pears, perhaps dotted with some tiny bunches of dark grapes, or a platter of peeled oranges sprinkled with rosewater, cinnamon and sugar, as would be the custom in the Arab countries and the 'coast of Barbary'.

Meals usually end with fruit rather than puddings. Fruit is added to wine to enhance its bouquet, like the Spanish *sangria*, and is also just dipped in the wine. As a child in Greece I was allowed to have some of my parents' wine when slices of peeled apples were added to it, as if this introduction lessened its alcoholic content and rendered it more suitable for a child's beverage.

Some summers ago, at a waterfront restaurant in Palermo in Sicily, under a starlit sky and among the rancid smell of decaying boats, we were offered by the proprietor a most generous dark terracotta jug filled with his own red wine and peeled slices of the most tantalizing and juiciest peaches.

I will never forget the spell of that drink or ever reproduce and catch its magical flavours.

Furthermore, fruit is pressed into revitalizing juices, it is liquidized into creamy, whirling delicious drinks and, in Greece, it is added to wholesome sheep's yoghurt, producing the most unexpectedly glorious combinations.

There is a great tradition of candying fruit, or its blossom, all around the Mediterranean, particularly exquisite in France, Italy and Spain; or preserving it in jars filled with cognac. On the eastern shores, there is a flurry of activity by the local women each season as they prepare their honey-coloured, sugar-dripping, spoon preserves. Green walnuts studded with an almond and the fragrance of a clove, unripe green figs, tiny aubergines, morello cherries, fresh green pistachio nuts and grapes are all used as the summer settles in; bitter oranges and bergamots in the autumn; orange or rose petals in the spring.

More amateur bottlings and distillations, some non-alcoholic like the Turkish and Arab sherbet which are left to mature in the hot summer sun, are tried by Levantines, Greeks and Turks, with cherries, peaches or apricots and their kernels. Lastly, there is the wealth of Moroccan meat dishes cooked with various fruits, collectively named as *touajen*. Originating in Persia, this tradition reached Morocco through the Arab invasions and also influenced the people of the eastern shores on its way.

Tarta de Naranja
Orange Custard

SPAIN

Richly fruity, while smooth and light, this is surely how Mediterranean desserts should taste. This is the winter equivalent of the summer *granita* (see overleaf).

195

300ml (10fl oz) fresh orange juice, unstrained but
   with pips removed (4 large oranges)
170g (6oz) sugar
150ml (5fl oz) water
5 egg yolks
1 egg

In a large saucepan, combine the orange juice, sugar and water, bring to the boil and boil gently for 7 minutes, until it thickens lightly. Let it cool for 10 minutes. In a large bowl, beat the egg yolks and the egg lightly, and slowly add the orange syrup, beating at the same time, until it has all been incorporated. Empty into a lightly buttered, small soufflé dish and cook in a *bain-marie* (place it in the middle of a larger oven dish with some hot water in it) in a preheated oven, gas no. 3 (325°F/160°C), for 35–40 minutes, until set. Serve hot.

Granita di Pesche

Peach Granita

This is the best *granita* for me. Made with ripe, sweet peaches at the height of the summer and eaten on a hot evening, there is nothing to compete with its smooth taste and exotic fragrance.

If the fruit used is not ripe enough, it should be immersed for 1–2 minutes in a bowl of boiling water to soften it, and then peeled.

675g (1½lb) peaches, peeled and stone removed
2 tablespoons lemon juice
170g (6oz) sugar
150ml (5fl oz) water

Liquidize the peaches with the lemon juice to prevent discolouring. In a saucepan, dissolve the sugar in the water and boil for 4–5 minutes until thickened, then cool. When completely cool, mix with the peaches and freeze. Take out of the freezer and whisk twice at 15-minute intervals to obtain a smooth and crystal-free texture. Remove from the freezer 10 minutes before it is to be served.

Kabak Tatlisi
A Pumpkin Dessert

TURKEY

Brilliantly coloured and sugary sweet, this is one of the most favoured autumnal desserts in Turkey. You can use toasted hazelnuts or almonds instead of the walnuts.

Serves 6

1kg (2lb) pumpkin, peeled and de-seeded
225g (8oz) sugar
225ml (8fl oz) double cream, whipped with 1
   tablespoon caster sugar
85g (3oz) coarsely chopped walnuts

Slice the pumpkin in thick, small pieces and layer it with the sugar in a saucepan. Leave overnight. It will have produced its own juices by the next day. Cover and simmer very slowly for about 2 hours, checking occasionally in case it dries out. It should be quite dry, soft, thick and sugary by the end of cooking time. Serve it covered with the whipped cream and walnuts.

Clafouti
A Cherry Flan

Clafouti is a popular dessert served at family meals during the cherry season in Limousin. Although the traditional *clafouti* is made with cherries, other fruits can be used successfully; plums, apricots, pears and peaches all make excellent alternatives. Larger fruit of this kind, however, are better rinsed and briefly poached first, for one minute at most. Then strain, peel, halve and stone the fruit (peeling plums or apricots is not necessary unless preferred). In addition, peaches and pears should be quartered or sliced thickly. Then proceed as for cherries.

Serves 4—6

BATTER

3 eggs
85g (3oz) sugar
55g (2oz) plain flour, sifted
1 teaspoon pure vanilla essence
Pinch of salt
425ml (15fl oz) milk

FILLING

450g (1lb) stoned black cherries *or* 560g (1¼lb)
  other fruit as above
1 tablespoon caster sugar
1 tablespoon icing sugar for sprinkling on top

Place all the batter ingredients in a liquidizer or food processor and blend for 1–2 minutes until perfectly smooth. Alternatively, if making by hand, beat the eggs and sugar, add the flour, vanilla, salt and a little milk and beat until smooth; lastly, add the remaining milk and beat until incorporated.

Spread the raw cherries, or any other prepared fruit, in one layer, in a lightly-buttered medium-sized, shallow [4cm(1½in)] baking dish and sprinkle the caster sugar over them. Pour over the batter and bake in a preheated oven, gas no. 5 (375°F/190°C), for 35–40 minutes until quite risen and golden on top.

Serve hot or warm and dust its top with the icing sugar just before serving.

Baklavas

GREECE/TURKEY

Baklava was first mentioned by the second-century AD Greek writer Athinaeos, who came from the Greek colony of Nafkratis in Egypt – near modern-day Alexandria. It has been adopted, varied and perfected since, by most countries all over the Middle East. Despite its mystique, it is easy to make and also suitable for a large gathering. All you need to master is the use of the ready-made Greek *fyllo* pastry, which is paper-thin (see page 64).

The following quantities will make about 14 pieces, and one should perhaps allow 2 per person. Store them, covered, at room temperature. They will keep for days although they may become a little drier.

PASTRY

450g (1lb) *fyllo* pastry (1 packet)
140g (5oz) unsalted butter, melted

FILLING

340—400g (12—14oz) walnuts, chopped coarsely
3 tablespoons sugar
½ teaspoon cinnamon

SYRUP

250g (9oz) sugar
360ml (12fl oz) water
2.5cm (1in) piece cinnamon stick
1 teaspoon lemon juice
2 tablespoons aromatic honey

Let the pastry defrost in its packet at room temperature. It will take about two hours. Do not remove from the packet as it will dry out and become brittle.

Mix all the filling ingredients in a bowl.

Choose an oblong roasting tin, approximately 38 x 26cm (15 x 10in); measure it against the stack of pastry and trim the pastry lengthways, allowing a little extra as it shrinks once cooked. Butter the base of the tin and line it neatly with 5 sheets of pastry, buttering each layer before lifting it from the stack. Spread half of the filling evenly over the pastry; cover with 4 more layers of buttered *fyllo* and spread the rest of the filling over. Fold over all edges, trapping the filling neatly, and then cover with the remaining pastry, buttering each layer first as before. Cut off excess pastry round the edges, so that it fits the dish neatly. Using a sharp knife, cut the top layers of the *baklava*, without cutting through to the base, into small square or diamond portions. (This will make it easier to serve, as it becomes tricky to cut *fyllo* neatly once it is cooked.)

Using the tips of your fingers, sprinkle a little cold water over the pastry to prevent the edges curling up, then cook in a preheated oven, gas no. 4 (350°F/180°C), for 25 minutes; turn up the heat to gas no. 5 (375°F/190°C) and cook for a further 10 minutes until light golden. Take out and allow to cool slightly.

To make the syrup, in a saucepan, dissolve the sugar in the water, add the cinnamon stick and lemon juice and boil for 5 minutes. Mix in the honey and simmer for a further 5 minutes, until lightly thickened. Let it cool slightly then discard the cinnamon stick and pour the syrup slowly over the *baklava*. Let it stand for 10 minutes in order to absorb

the syrup and become moist. Cut and remove the pieces
individually.

Granita di Caffè
Coffee Ice

Coffee, although not grown in the Mediterranean, is
indisputably part of Mediterranean life. And since one cannot
go to Italy and not sip a coffee ice at an outdoor café in
a stuccoed square, this recipe had to be included.

Espresso coffee as made in Italy is unmatched anywhere
else. Not any odd brew, bitter from over-roasted beans,
espresso is not so-named because of its dark colour and
bitterness, but it is the blend of the coffee that matters.
My favourite place for drinking and buying their special
house blends of espresso is the Palombini Coffee House in
Via Po near the Vatican.

If an espresso blend is not available, any freshly-made
strong coffee will do.

> 600ml (1 pint) freshly-made strong coffee of
> fragrant variety (my own favourite blend is 3
> parts of Kenya Pale Peaberry mixed with 1 part
> of Creole)
> 6 tablespoons sugar
> 150ml (5fl oz) whipped cream made with equal
> parts of single and double cream and 1 tablespoon
> caster sugar

Make the coffee by one of the filter methods and, while
it is hot, dissolve the sugar in it. Let it cool and then put
in the freezer. Take out and whisk twice at 15-minute
intervals in order to obtain a smooth texture. Remove from

the freezer 10 minutes before it is to be served and serve with some whipped cream on top.

DRINKS

Kaysi Sherbet

Apricot Sherbet

TURKEY

This delicious home-made drink is the one most commonly served in Turkish homes, particularly the traditional households where alcohol is forbidden. The most exquisite version was served to us after a luscious lunch in the garden of the home of Mr Niyazi Ildirar, in Konya, during the International Food Congress in Turkey recently.

1kg (2lb) sweet, ripe apricots, washed and stoned
4 tablespoons water
450g (1lb) sugar

Place the apricots and water in a large saucepan, bring to the boil, cover and simmer for about 15 minutes, until quite soft. Press through a sieve to remove the apricot skins. Measure the fruit, with a teacup perhaps, add twice its volume in sugar and place back in the saucepan. Mix well and simmer until sugar has completely dissolved. Test for setting point by placing a teaspoon of the mixture onto a very cold plate; wait a minute then push the mixture with your finger and if it wrinkles setting point has been reached. If not, continue cooking a little longer and repeat the process. Let it cool a little, pour into sterilized jars and seal. (The lady in Istanbul who gave me this recipe seals the bottles around their corks using wax and they will then keep for up to two years.)

Store in a cool cupboard. To serve, place 3–4 tablespoons of sherbet in each glass and dilute with cold water.

Ayran
Yoghurt Drink

Ayran is the most popular drink offered with meals in Turkey. In Syria and the Lebanon it is called *laban* and it is a particularly excellent accompaniment to a vegetable meal, with its refreshing but also satisfying qualities.

> **225g (8oz) thick sheep's yoghurt such as the Greek variety**
> **150ml (5fl oz) cold water**
> **A little salt**
> **A pinch of dried mint**

Place all the ingredients, except the mint, in a food processor or blender and blend for 1–2 minutes until smooth and lightly frothy. Serve chilled in long glasses with a hint of mint on top.

Alternatively, beat in a bowl with an egg whisker until well amalgamated, chill and serve as before.

BIBLIOGRAPHY

Apicius de re Quoquinaria, 1498, *The Roman Cookery Book*, translated by Barbara Flower and Elisabeth Rosenbaum, George G. Harrap & Co., London 1958

Arberry, Professor A.J., 'A Baghdad cookery book', translated in *The Islamic Culture*, 1939

Aristophanes, *The Frogs*, 'Ekklisiazousae', translated by Patrick Dickinson, Oxford University Press, London 1970

Belloc, Hilaire, 'Ladies and Gentlemen' from *Cautionary Verses*, Duckworth, London 1940

Boni, Ada, *Italian Regional Cooking*, Godfrey Cave, London 1982

Braudel, Fernand, *The Mediterranean and the Mediterranean World in the Age of Philip II*, Fontana, London 1981

Brothwell, Don and Patricia, *Food in Antiquity*, Thames & Hudson, London 1969

Caruana Galizia, Anne and Helen, *Recipes from Malta*, Progress Press Co. Ltd, Malta 1979

Davidson, Alan, *Mediterranean Seafood*, Penguin, London 1981

Dioskoridis, *The Greek Herbal*, translated by John Goodyer, New York 1655, edited and first printed by Robert T. Gunther, Oxford 1933

Douglas, Norman, *Siren Land*, Secker & Warburg, London 1957

  South Wind, Secker & Warburg, London 1947

Ford, Richard, *Gatherings from Spain*, London 1846

Goethe, 'Mignonslied' from *Selected Verse*, edited by D. Duke, Penguin, London 1964

Haroutunian, Arto der, *North African Cookery*, Century, London 1985

Kavafi, Constantine, *Poems*, translated by John
  Mavrokordato, Chatto & Windus, London 1971
Koukoules, Professor Phaidon, *ΒΥΖΑΝΤΙΝΩΝ ΒΙΟΣ ΚΑΙ
  ΠΟΛΙΤΙΣΜΟΣ*, Collection de l'Institut Français
  d'Athènes. ΑθΗΝΑ 1948
  *ΒΥΖΑΝΤΙΝΩ ΤΡΟøΑΙ ΚΑΙ ΠΟΤΑ' ΕΠΕΤΗΡΙΣ
  ΕΤΑΙΡΕΙΑΣΒΥΖΑΝΤΙΝΩΝ ΣΠΟΥΔΩΝ*, ΑθΗΝΑ 1941
Miha-Lambaki, Aspasia, *Η ΔΙΑΤΡΟøΗ ΤΩΝ ΑΡΧΑΙΩΝ
  ΕΛΛΗΝΩΝ ΚΑΤΑ ΤΟΥΣ ΑΡΧΑΙΟΥΣ
  ΚΩΜΩΔΙΟΓΡΑøΟΥΣ*, ΑθΗΝΑ 1984
Pananti, Signor, *Narrative of a residence in Algiers*, translated
  by E. Blanquiere, London 1818
Perry, Charles, 'Buran: 1100 Years in the Life of a Dish'
  from *The Journal of Gastronomy*, Vol. I, California 1984
Pezzini, Wilma, *Tuscan Cookbook*, Dent, London 1979
Plato, *Republic*, translated by Paul Shorey, Loeb Classical
  Library, William Heinemann, London 1930
Roden, Claudia, *A Book of Middle Eastern Food*, Penguin,
  London 1976
Root, Waverley, *The Food of France*, Random House, Vintage
  Books, New York 1977
Runciman, Sir Steven, *A History of the Crusades*, Penguin,
  Peregrine Books, London 1980
Salaman, Rena, *Greek Food*, Fontana, London 1983
Salt, H.S., *Flesh or Fruit*, an essay on Food Reform, 1886
Shelley, *Shelley, Selected Poetry, Prose and Letters*, edited by
  A.S.B. Glover, Nonesuch Library Edition, London 1951
Smollett, Tobias, *Travels through France and Italy*, R. Baldwin,
  London 1766
Spanish Women's Institute, *Cocina Regional Española*, Madrid
  1976
Turabi, Effendi, *A Turkish Cookery Book*, London 1862
Weber, Eugen, *Peasants into Frenchmen*, Chatto & Windus,
  London 1979, first published by Stamford University
  Press, 1976
Willan, Anne, *French Regional Cooking*, Hutchinson, London
  1981

INDEX